# Teachers with Class

# TEACHERS *with* CLASS

*True Stories of Great Teachers*

MARSHA SERLING GOLDBERG and SONIA FELDMAN

**Andrews McMeel
Publishing**

Kansas City

03 04 05 06 07 RR2 10 9 8 7 6 5 4 3 2 1

ISBN: 0-7407-3323-0

Library of Congress Cataloging-in-Publication Data

Goldberg, Marsha Serling.
    Teachers with class: true stories of great teachers / Marsha Serling Goldberg and Sonia Feldman.
       p. cm.
    Includes bibliographical references and index.
    ISBN 0-7407-3323-0
       1. Teacher-student relationships—United States—Anecdotes. 2. Teachers—United States—Anecdotes. 3. Teaching—Awards—United States. I. Feldman, Sonia. II. Title.

    LB1033 .G58 2003
    371.1—dc21

                                        2002034524

---

**ATTENTION: SCHOOLS AND BUSINESSES**
Andrews McMeel books are available at quantity discounts with bulk purchase for educational, business, or sales promotional use. For information, please write to: Special Sales Department, Andrews McMeel Publishing, 4520 Main Street, Kansas City, Missouri 64111.

---

Book Design by Desiree Mueller

**THE NEA FOUNDATION**
FOR THE IMPROVEMENT
*of* EDUCATION

*T*he NEA Foundation for the Improvement of Education (NFIE) highly commends *Teachers with Class* to everyone who works in public education. Created by the members of the National Education Association (NEA), the NEA Foundation empowers public education employees to innovate, take risks, and become agents for change to improve teaching and learning in our society. The foundation provides a variety of grants, awards, free publications, and resources for U.S. public educators.

*A portion of the proceeds of this book will be donated to the NEA Foundation.*

**For more information about the foundation, please contact:**

**The NEA Foundation**
**for the Improvement of Education**
**1201 Sixteenth Street, NW**
**Washington, DC 20036-3207**
**Telephone 202-822-7840**
**Facsimile 202-822-7779**
**www.nfie.org**

*We dedicate this book with love to
our husbands, Jerry Feldman and Linn Goldberg,
and our children, Ben and Alie Feldman,
Gabe, Andrew, Aaron, Michael, and Alex Goldberg.*

*We adore each and every one of you and
are so grateful for your support and humor
as we worked on this enriching project.*

*In loving memory of Judith Kenez.*

*Presented to :*

*The most important day*
*I remember in all my life*
*is the one in which*
*my teacher came to me.*

**— Helen Keller**

# Contents

# Acknowledgments

This book exists because of the heartfelt contributions of so many people. When your stories arrived by letter, fax, and e-mail, it was a joy and a privilege to read them. While space prohibits us from including every story we received, we are indebted to all of you for your gift of time and expression, and hope that each of you will contact your teachers to let them know how much they touched your lives.

Gabe, thank you for literally running around Manhattan for us. Margie, thank you for putting your red pen to paper and helping us edit our edits all the way from your desk in Yokne'am Ilit, Israel. Diane, Sally, Lorraine, Gigi, Sandi, Angie, Rick, Leigh, Kathy, Carla, Peggy, and Ted, thank you for your support.

Grateful appreciation to Peter Miller from PMA Literary and Film Management, Inc., and Jean Lucas from Andrews McMeel for your hard work and dedication to our project. Thank you to Judith Renyi, Executive Director of the NEA Foundation; Ann Weinheimer from the Department of Education, and Jan Burgess and Pete Lorain for your guidance and enthusiasm.

With so much love, we thank the very first teachers in our lives, our parents: Judith Kenez, Helen and Jacob Serling, and Allan and Annette Hackner.

We gratefully honor and thank our own teachers with class: H. Charles Hill from the University of Vermont; Dr. Lorraine Davis and Dr. Richard Schlaadt from the University of Oregon; Terah Kathryn Collins, Jonathan Hulsh, Becky Iott, Brian Collins, and Ellen Schneider from the Western School of Feng Shui in Solana Beach, California; and Ronald J. Smetanick from Thomas W. Pyle Junior High School in Bethesda, Maryland, who put up with our giggles and antics in eighth-grade science class as our friendship blossomed. ❧

mary anne mbl radmacher©

people ask,
"why do you work
so hard for
your students?".
there are so many
things i could say
but the
answer must be—

because of one child.

i swim through seas of papers with colored pens as paddles - seeking to improve without dispiriting, to point a better way without losing their enthusiasm.

**because of one child** i seek my own reserves and provide opportunities which would otherwise be lost.

because of one child i will spend my time generously - as if i had a lifetime of such days. i will see the whole of the world from a small hill and will believe, against convention, in "impossible" results

at the end of the teaching day i leave the classroom but i am still, and shall ever be, a teacher. time ago i was that child for whom such commitment made a difference. i will dedicate my days confident my efforts matter . . .

. . . because of one child.

PLEASE SEE MS. RADMACHER'S STORY ON PAGE 112.

# Introduction

We decided to collaborate on a book about teachers with class for several reasons.

One morning last fall amidst a rather typical scenario in her house, Marsha's husband, Linn, fed their dog, Benson; gobbled a quick bite himself; kissed everyone good-bye; then dashed out the door for the University Hospital in Portland, Oregon, where he works as a physician. Two of their five sons grabbed protein bars and homework assignments and raced out the door after him to go to school. All very routine.

What made this morning eventful for Marsha, however, was the copy of the October 18 *Newsweek* on their kitchen counter left open to a piece by Robert Samuelson entitled: "The Gift of a Great Teacher."

"Read this, Mom. You'll love it." was written on the attached Post-it note by their eighteen-year-old son, Aaron. She did *and* she did. (Read it, that is, and love it.) This inspiring essay, which appears in its entirety on page seven, begins "If you are lucky in life, you will have at least one great teacher."

Marsha thought about the essay all morning. She thought about the teachers in her life who impacted her greatly. She thought about the exemplary teachers in our children's lives, about Morrie in *Tuesdays with Morrie* and how this beautiful and simple book by Mitch Album continues to touch the hearts of millions.

On the other side of the country in Annapolis, Maryland, Sonia was organizing her desk and came across a copy of the book she had made to give to her children's teachers as an end of the year remembrance. In an effort to give something that would be more meaningful than yet another coffee mug, Sonia organized the children in the classes and had each of them write a paragraph about what he/she liked most about the teachers. What better gift to give a teacher (other than perhaps a pay raise!) than feedback, acknowledgment, and appreciation from the students for everything their teachers taught them? Sonia recalled how much the students loved writing their stories and how moved the teachers had been by them. The phone rang. . . .

Marsha called Sonia, her close friend since their junior high days in Bethesda, Maryland, and asked her to find her copy of the latest *Newsweek*, read the piece by Robert Samuelson, and call her back. She did both. And so this project began.

We talked about a way to honor great teachers, and decided to collect stories for a book. We wrote, e-mailed, faxed, phoned, and interviewed "famous" and "not so famous" folks and asked if they had a "special teacher story." The response was overwhelmingly positive!

What follows are the stories we hope will spark a memory about the special teacher in your own life—the one who influenced you in a meaningful way. Maybe it was her enthusiasm for a certain subject that triggered your own joy of learning, or maybe it was his ability to reach you at a time in your life when you felt particularly unreachable. If you weren't fortunate enough to be taught by one really great teacher, we bet you know one . . . a colleague, a friend, an aunt, or your child's teacher. We all know teachers who inspire, open minds, stimulate, and motivate students. You can acknowledge him or her by writing a note of thanks.

In addition, we have included a partial list of Grants and Awards available to teachers. To really say "thank you," you may wish to refer to this list and nominate your own teacher with class!

And now, sit back, read and enjoy *Teachers with Class.* ❧

*— Marsha Serling Goldberg and Sonia Feldman*

# *Robert J. Samuelson*

Robert Samuelson began his journalism career as a reporter on the *Washington Post*'s business desk in 1969. After four years he left the paper to freelance. His articles were published by the *Sunday Times* of London, the *Los Angeles Times*, the *Boston Globe*, the *New Republic*, and other publications. He joined the *National Journal* as an economics correspondent in 1976 and began writing its "Economic Focus" column. He started writing a column for the *Washington Post* in 1977 and joined *Newsweek* as a contributing editor in 1984. He joined the Washington Post Writers Group in January 1996.

Samuelson was born in New York City. He is a 1967 graduate of Harvard with a B.A. in government. He resides in Bethesda, Maryland, with his wife Judith and three children.

In 1997, he was a finalist for the Gerald Loeb Award for Distinguished Business and Financial Journalism for commentary. The *Washingtonian* magazine named him among the top fifty journalists in the capital city the same year.

ROBERT J. SAMUELSON'S TEACHER WITH CLASS IS
## ❧ PROFESSOR EDWARD C. BANFIELD

# Professor Edward C. Banfield

*I*f you are lucky in life, you will have at least one great teacher. More than three decades ago, I had Ed Banfield, a political scientist who taught mainly at the University of Chicago and Harvard University. Ed's recent death at eighty-three saddened me (which was expected) and left me with a real sense of loss (which wasn't). Although we had stayed in touch, we were never intimate friends or intellectual soulmates. The gap between us in intellectual candlepower was too great. But he had loomed large in my life, and I have been puzzling why his death has so affected me.

I think the answer—and the reason for writing about something so personal—goes to the heart of what it means to be a great teacher. By teacher, I am not referring primarily to classroom instructors, because learning in life occurs mainly outside of schools. I first encountered Ed in a lecture hall, but his greatness did not lie in giving good lectures (which he did). It lay instead in somehow transmitting life-changing lessons. If I had not known him, I would be a different person. He helped me become who I am and, more important, who I want to be.

When you lose someone like that, there is a hole. It is a smaller hole than losing a parent, a child or close friend. But it is still a hole, because great teachers are so rare. I have, for example, worked for some very talented editors. A few have earned my lasting gratitude for improving my reporting or writing. But none has been a great teacher; none has changed my life.

What gave Ed this power was, first, his ideas. He made me see new things or old things in new ways. The political scientist James Q. Wilson—first Ed's student, then his collaborator—has called Banfield "the most profound student of American politics in this century." Although arguable, this is surely plausible.

Americans take democracy, freedom and political stability for granted. Ed was more wary. These great things do not exist in isolation. They must somehow fuse into a political system that fulfills certain essential social functions: to protect the nation; to provide some continuity in government and policy; to maintain order and modulate society's most passionate conflicts. The trouble, Ed believed, is that democracies have certain self-destructive tendencies and that, in modern America, these had intensified.

On the whole, he regretted the disappearance after World War II of a political system based on big-city machines (whose supporters were rewarded with patronage jobs and contracts) and on party "bosses" (who dictated political candidates from city council to Congress and, often, the White House). It was not that he favored patronage, corruption or bosses for their own sake. But in cities, they created popular support for government and gave it the power to accomplish things. And they emphasized material gain over ideological fervor.

Postwar suburbanization and party "reforms"—weakening bosses and machines—destroyed this system. Its replacement, Ed feared, was inferior. "Whereas the old system had promised personal rewards," he wrote, "the new one promises social reform." Politicians would now merchandise themselves by selling false solutions to exaggerated problems. "The politician, like the TV news commentator, must always have something to say even when nothing urgently needs to be said," he wrote in 1970. By several decades, this anticipated the term, "talking head." People would lose respect for government because many "solutions" would fail. Here, too, he anticipated. Later, polls showed dropping public confidence in national leaders. Ed was not surprised.

He taught that you had to understand the world as it is, not as you wished it to be. This was sound advice for an aspiring reporter. And Ed practiced it. In 1954 and 1955, he and his wife, Laura (they would ultimately be married sixty-one years), spent time in a poor Italian village to explain its poverty. The resulting book—*The Moral Basis of a Backward Society*—remains a classic. Families in the village, it argued, so distrusted each other that they could not cooperate to promote common prosperity. The larger point (still missed by many economists) is that local culture, not just "markets," determines economic growth.

What brought Ed fleeting prominence—notoriety, really—was *The Unheavenly City*. Published in 1970, it foretold the failure of the War on Poverty. Prosperity, government programs and less racial discrimination might lift some from poverty, he said. But the worst problems of poverty and cities would remain. They resulted from a "lower class" whose members were so impulsive and "present oriented" that they attached "no value to work, sacrifice, self-improvement, or service to family, friends or community." They dropped out of school, had illegitimate children and were unemployed. Government couldn't easily alter their behavior.

For this message, Ed was reviled as a reactionary. He repeatedly said that most black Americans didn't belong to the "lower class" and that it contained many whites. Still, many dismissed him as a racist. Over time, his theories gained some respectability from the weight of experience. Poverty defied government assaults; his "lower class" was relabeled "the underclass." But when he wrote, Ed was assailing prevailing opinion. He knew he would be harshly, even viciously, attacked. He wrote anyway and endured the consequences.

This was the deeper lesson. Perhaps all great teachers—whether parents, bosses, professors or whoever—ultimately convey some moral code. Ed surely did. What he was saying in the 1960s was not what everyone else was saying. I felt uneasy with the reigning orthodoxy. But I didn't know why. Ed helped me understand my doubts and made me feel that it was important to give them expression. The truth had to be pursued, no matter how inconvenient, unpopular, unfashionable or discomforting. Ed did not teach that; he lived it. This was his code, and it was—for anyone willing to receive it—an immeasurable gift. ✿

*Those having torches
will pass them on to others.*

— **Plato**


*Much I have learned
from my teachers,
more from my colleagues,
but most from my students.*

— **Talmud**

# Susan Bladholm

Susan Bladholm, a native Oregonian, jumps at any opportunity that distinctly benefits her home state. Projects include cofounding and directing Cycle Oregon (a weeklong annual bicycle tour), staging events internationally to promote the state, and executive producing a music CD to raise funds for the local children's science museum. Her "biggest" client to date was Keiko the whale, from the movie *Free Willy.* A mother of two who fundraises for children's charities in Portland, she is currently serving as Marketing and Communications Manager for the Port of Portland.

SUSAN BLADHOLM'S TEACHER WITH CLASS IS
❦ **MR. FRANK CASTILLO**

# MR. FRANK CASTILLO

At Cedar Park Junior High, I was the geeky six-foot-tall bookworm who only left the security of the library to bat the ball on the tennis court. I met Mr. Franklin Castillo in my eighth-grade Civil Rights Class.

You knew immediately that things were a bit different in his class. If you acted out in class, you were sent out to the hall to look for camels. (To this day his camel collection exceeds one hundred.) You never asked what grade you got. You asked what grade you earned. Also, you could gamble your test score by wagering that your answers (most in essay format) were all spelled correctly. If you were correct, you were given a bonus of several points. If you were wrong, the number of points you had "lost" due to incorrect or incomplete answers was doubled.

In Civil Rights, a mock trial was held and I was elected as judge. Mr. Castillo sat in the back of the room with flash cards for me that indicated "overruled" or "I'll allow it." After a day I overruled him and was on my own making decisions for the remainder of the class.

Since those days in the late '70s when I took every class that he offered, we have stayed in touch and made it a practice of getting together at least once a year. He and his wife now reside at a retirement center in Portland and, as I could have predicted, have maintained their buoyant sense of humor and zest for life. During our last visit they must have introduced our family to at least two hundred people. Frank leads the bridge club (they are accomplished players), and Florence swims, and power walks the resident pooch. They both tend a beautiful garden of Portland roses.

I believe that there are guardian angels that come into our lives that we don't recognize as such at the time. Frank Castillo was certainly one of mine. Frank (although at thirty-four years of age I still often call my eighty-six-year-old friend "Mr. Castillo") instilled much-needed confidence in me, pushed me to be my best, and always let me know that I was special. Even after I lost to the smarmy little twit on our tennis team, he sat me down and told me why I would win the next time. Fortunately for me, he was right, as always.

I could write all day about him. I didn't care much what class he was teaching, I knew I would be the better for it by just being in his class.

Mr. Castillo attended the College of Puget Sound through 1937. I graduated from the renamed University of Puget Sound in 1987.

Two phrases Mr. Castillo posted on his bulletin board that I will always remember were:

"A preposition is a poor word to end a sentence with.

And never begin a sentence with a conjunction." ❤

*Teaching is the most
responsible, the least advertised,
the worst paid, and the most
richly rewarded profession
in the world.*

**— Ian Hay**

# Senator Gordon Smith

Mr. Smith went to Washington to be sworn in as United States Senator from Oregon on January 7, 1997. Not only did he become effective in working with Senate leadership to pass legislation benefiting Oregon, but he also has become known for his ability to cross party lines in the interests of his constituents. He was selected twice as Deputy Whip of the Senate and is a member of four major committees: Energy and Natural Resources, Foreign Relations, Budget, and the Commerce, Science, and Transportation committee.

Born May 25, 1952, in Pendleton, Oregon, Senator Smith graduated from Brigham Young University in 1976 and earned a law degree from Southwestern University in 1979. After working as an attorney in private practice, Smith assumed management of his family's frozen vegetable processing company, a position he held until his election to the U.S. Senate. He began his political life when he was elected to the Oregon State Senate in 1992 and became president of the State Senate during his first term in office. Senator Smith and his wife, Sharon, have three children, Brittany, Garrett, and Morgan. They maintain homes in Bethesda, Maryland, and Pendleton, Oregon.

GORDON SMITH'S TEACHER WITH CLASS IS
## &. MR. COOK

# Mr. Cook

*I* was a boy of big dreams and too many daydreams. Mr. Cook saw in me the possibility of putting forth more effort and turning my dreams into reality. He was my teacher at Radnor Elementary School in Bethesda, Maryland.

He came to my home, talked to me of my dreams, and taught me how to make them come true. He was interested in politics and I was from a political family. Even after the school year came to an end, we continued to share our bond of friendship and mutual interest. He continued to teach me all summer long so that I would be better prepared for Junior High School. I do not remember all the lessons or subjects that he taught me, but I do remember that he cared about me and helped me. I will never forget him or cease to be grateful to him. ❧

# Brian Dutra

After graduating from the University of Oregon, Brian did what most graduates do with a degree in Social Sciences/English; he went to New York and sang opera. While singing in New York, he continued writing, sold his blue suede couch, and ended up in Los Angeles, doing commercials for clients such as Oldsmobile, Ocean Spray, United Way, and Protection One. He also worked in the film division of the Walt Disney Company. After leaving Disney, he became an independent writer and proofer/editor of film and television for the international market. He met his wife, Sally, in Los Angeles when she was performing in the improv company Just Kidding. As a writing team, Brian and Sally have had film projects optioned by Warner Bros., Paramount, and Motown.

BRIAN DUTRA'S TEACHER WITH CLASS IS
∾ MRS. HITCHCOCK

# Mrs. Hitchcock

*I*f one hundred people boarded a train in California heading to New York and every 156 miles two people get off, how many people would be left on the train when it reached its New York destination?

My answer has never changed—why get off the train before New York and miss out on all the good eats that you paid for? Only a colossal moron would do that! It was obvious to even my sixth-grade self that a math career was not in my future. And, even though I hadn't a nodule of interest in this field, I was upset. My older brother was stellar in math and basketball. I played basketball like football and math was like a foreign language. I would never be better than my big brother at anything. I was destined to become a bum.

But, lo and behold, Mrs. Hitchcock appeared in my life. A sixth-grade teaching angel. Mrs. Hitchcock felt that my affinity for the bizarre and dramatic would be better utilized in writing and performing. This was most definitely an earth-shattering fireworks concept to me. I had already accepted being weird as a legitimate avocation that would remain as such. The idea that it could be used to my advantage was pure genius. Mrs. Hitchcock was a bona fide, ass-kickin' Einstein. With herculean effort she encouraged me to enter my first writing contest. I did and I won. And in my moment of supreme glory, I recited my composition to the entire school . . . with my zipper down. So much for escaping my past. But Mrs. Hitchcock encouraged me to move forward. She declared my writing so brilliant that the students were listening too intently and were too busy digesting my innovative thoughts to even notice the errant zipper.

I believed Mrs. Hitchcock then and if she were sitting in front of me now, I would still believe her. That's how good she was. Thank you, Mrs. Hitchcock, wherever you are! I'm only a bum on weekends now, and I think that's okay. ❧

*"Mr. P" (Frank Pignata), my seventh-grade geometry and computer teacher, was a taskmaster, but he did it with love and a real commitment to growing children into responsible adults. I remember he once stayed after class to go over some of the problems I got wrong. I just got the feeling there wasn't a day that passed that he wasn't happy with what he was doing.*

**— Jane Clayson, cohost of CBS's The Early Show**

# *Sally Dutra*

Growing up in Park Ridge, Illinois, gave Sally the opportunity to study improvisational comedy at Second City in Chicago. After high school she traveled west to U.C.L.A. and graduated with a B.A. degree in theater, dance, music, and film. She then studied more improv with The Groundlings in Los Angeles. She has performed stand-up comedy at the Ice House in Pasadena and the Comedy Store in Los Angeles, as well as playing improvisational games with the children at the Ronald McDonald House in Los Angeles (by far her favorite crowd). Currently, she has combined her love of comedy and children by writing a comic, sci-fi middle reader novel. She is also a member of the Society of Children's Book Writers and Illustrators.

SALLY DUTRA'S TEACHER WITH CLASS IS
**❦ MR. DON MARTELLO**

# MR. DON MARTELLO

*T*he year was 1974. I was a freshman at Maine South High in Park Ridge, Illinois. My older, prettier, popular, pompom-toting sister, Mary, was a confident senior. I was a nervous, insecure, and frightened freshman. After all, this was high school. With sweaty palms, a brown suede skirt, and a bright yellow ruffled blouse I entered the imposing school, all the while trembling on the inside.

Who was I? And what did I hope to gain out of my high school experience? Beats me.

I did know that I was willing to try new things. My sister was on the synchronized swim team, so I tried out too. I was confident that a summer of practicing "ballet leg" was sure to get me in. It did not. I was shattered as I read the list of names for the synchronized swim team. My name was not among them.

So I tried out for the Variety Show and that's when I met him. Mr. Don Martello—a drama teacher/director/mentor who would end up having a lifelong impact on me.

He was short and pudgy (like the Pillsbury Dough Boy with a goatee) and he was fond of sitting on a chair backward while directing a show or giving a lecture. He had a nervous "snort-sneeze" that would quietly slip out of his nose without warning, but instead of making us laugh somehow we all understood it had more to do with nerves than an actual medical condition.

Meeting Mr. Don Martello, working with him on the Variety Show, and later being in his class and working with him on other productions as a character, a lighting person, and an assistant director taught me so much about life and its beauty and passion.

With great compassion, brilliant insight, and a genuine kindness, Mr. Martello helped unlock a part of my soul and direct me in a lifelong pursuit. He built up my self-esteem by encouraging me to believe in myself and step forward in life to pursue my dreams. He was fond of saying "It will jell" during a production—meaning everything will come together in time for opening night.

Well, Mr. Martello, even though you are no longer here on this planet, I still want you to know that I am forever grateful for your impact and forever indebted for your spirit of generosity.

And I want you to know, it did jell and it's still jelling! ৯

*Genius without education
is like Silver in the Mine.*

— **Benjamin Franklin**


*A child miseducated
is a child lost.*

— **John Fitzgerald Kennedy**

# *James Earl Jones*

Celebrated actor James Earl Jones is known for his powerful and critically acclaimed motion picture, television, and theater performances. His performance in the Alan Paton classic *Cry, the Beloved Country*, promises to remain in the annals of acting studies that will be researched by students of the art throughout the years. He has been praised by critics for his award-winning performance in *A Family Thing*, a strong human drama that pairs him with Robert Duvall. For all of his success in television and the movies, Jones's beginnings are in the theater.

He earned worldwide acclaim and his first Tony award in the role of Jack Johnson, the first heavyweight boxing champion, in Howard Sackler's *The Great White Hope*. His second Tony came as a result of his stunning performance in August Wilson's play *Fences*. He has also received critical praise for his autobiography, *James Earl Jones: Voices and Silences*, which he coauthored with Penelope Niven.

In addition to a long career as a theater, film, and television actor, Jones is well known as the voice of CNN and Bell Atlantic and Darth Vader in the *Star Wars* movies. His deep, resonant voice is among the most recognizable in the country.

JAMES EARL JONES'S TEACHER WITH CLASS IS
## ❦ PROFESSOR DONALD CROUCH

# PROFESSOR DONALD CROUCH

*F*irst of all let me say I don't believe in mentors. That is, I don't believe that people can set out to be role models; if they do, it is usually somewhat false, and it doesn't work. For instance, a parent can't just decide to be a role model for his or her child. When such a relationship does exist, it usually just happens, because that child sees something in his role model which he responds to positively, which helps him search within himself to find his own potential.

I was raised by my grandparents, and I would say that my grandfather was, and still is, my hero. Outside of the family, my most influential role model was a high school English teacher, Donald Crouch. Professor Crouch was a former college teacher who had worked with Robert Frost, among others. He had retired to a farm near the small Michigan town where I lived, but when he discovered that there was a need for good teachers locally he came to teach at my small agricultural high school.

Growing up, I had a hard time speaking because I was a stutterer, and felt self-conscious. Professor Crouch discovered that I wrote poetry, a secret I was not anxious to divulge, being a typical high school boy. After learning this, he questioned me about why, if I loved words so much, couldn't I say them out loud? One day I showed him a poem I had written, and he responded to it by saying that it was too good to be my own work, that I must have copied it from someone. To prove that I hadn't plagiarized it, he wanted me to recite the poem, by heart, in front of the entire class. I did as he asked, got through it without stuttering, and from then on I had to write more, and speak more. This had a tremendous effect on me, and my confidence grew as I learned to express myself comfortably out loud.

On the last day of school, we had our final class outside on the lawn, and Professor Crouch presented me with a gift—a copy of Ralph Waldo Emerson's *Self-Reliance*. This was invaluable to me because it summed up what he had taught me—self-reliance. His influence on me was so basic that it extended to all areas of my life. He is the reason I became an actor. Several years later I was in Shakespeare's *Timon of Athens* at the Yale Repertory Theater.

Of course, Professor Crouch was the one person I knew I definitely had to invite, and so I asked him to come see me. By that time, though, he was almost completely blind, and said that he would rather not come if he couldn't see me. This was a disappointment, but I understood why he did not want to come, and knew that he was right. In terms of overall influence, he is still the most important person outside my family whose inspiration has helped and guided me over the years. 🕭

*I was only a little mass of possibilities. It was my teacher (Annie Sullivan) who unfolded and developed them. . . . She never since let pass an opportunity to make my life sweet and useful.*

**— Helen Keller**

# *James Holman*

James Holman is science editor of the *Oregonian* in Portland. He also has been a reporter, copy editor, and news editor at newspapers in Astoria and Eugene, Oregon; Vancouver, Washington; and San Diego, California, during his twenty-four-year career. He graduated from the University of Oregon and is proud to be a Duck.

His daughter, Kira, and son, Wyeth, inherited a gene that predisposes them to nearsightedness and a lifetime of burying their noses in books, but at the same time makes them oblivious to homework, chores, and other distractions.

JAMES HOLMAN'S TEACHER WITH CLASS IS
ﾟ▱ **MR. BOTT**

# MR. BOTT

*T*he word wriggled between the commas like a worm in a schoolboy's polished apple.

Essayist Christopher Hitchens had fenced it off, set it apart, whispered it in passing. Perhaps he hoped no one would notice. Or perhaps his editors at *Harper's* had bracketed the homely adverb, brazenly, never having had Mr. Bott's sure counsel. Had they been students in Richard Bott's high school English class, they would have been less brazen.

I remember nothing of the magazine article surrounding the word. It was a political polemic on neoconservatism, tangy but with no aftertaste. The flawed sentence was no more memorable, marred by the passive and freighted with excess. But suddenly, four words in, Mr. Bott appeared: a ghostly sentinel pacing the cramped classroom in his corduroy sport coat and chinos.

"It was argued, thusly, that this very ruthlessness . . ." the sentence in the *Harper's* piece began. It ran on for a dozen more unremarkable words, expressing no particularly noteworthy sentiment.

"Thusly," the author wrote. And thus, from my memory, he summoned Mr. Bott. Because of him, a metaphoric neon light, with commas to and fro, fairly beamed the nonword from the page. It was the very neologism that had beckoned me down my stumbling intellectual path, trackless though it sometimes since has seemed.

Mr. Bott surely would not remember. I do, though, as if it were months ago, rather than thirty years. If I rummaged through battered boxes carted along in Volkswagens, borrowed pickups, U-Hauls, and moving vans from dormitory to apartment to house to home, I might discover the original yellowed paper. It would be printed in a rather precise longhand and written in a sincere and sophomoric style (for I was, after all, a high school sophomore).

"Thusly," I wrote. Did I set it off with commas? I don't recall, nor do I recall the topic sentence of my "essay."

Three decades later, though, I still recall Mr. Bott's gentle correction. No such word, he noted matter-of-factly, after first offering praise for something I had done reasonably well. That was his way: positive reinforcement, constructive criticism, consistent standards, respect for all.

I'll never forget my sense of wonder that I could have coined a word. Pride in authorship, I suppose. The -ly seemed, and in an odd way still seems, logical.

Yet I never again used it, not once in twenty years of making my living with words. A lesson well-learned. I also never again used the plain but serviceable adverb "thus" without thinking of that youthful, extraneous -ly, and of Mr. Bott.

I see him before the sophomore English class, in that basement room next to the tray-clattering cafeteria. I see him frowning, adjusting his wire-rimmed glasses, running a hand through his hair, struggling to reach us. He was determined to impart to twenty semiliterate, ill-prepared, lazy, hopelessly naive, adolescent daydreamers something of value that might grow in us like a seed, if somehow we learned to water it.

Then to find "thusly" smirking from the pages of a well-edited magazine such as *Harper's*. I nearly took up my pen to write to those uncharacteristically careless editors, to chide them for nodding. For letting Mr. Bott down.

I would remind them to reread their Strunk and White, 3rd edition. There it is, on page 76 of the indispensable *Elements of Style*, in a typically Strunkian command: "Rule 12: Do not construct awkward adverbs. . . . Do not dress words up by adding *ly* to them, as though putting a hat on a horse." Then, this list of worldly temptations: "overly, muchly, thusly." Sound advice. I have tried these many years to avoid putting hats on my horses, difficult as that can be.

Somehow Mr. Bott got through to me. He taught me much more than an appreciation for the mechanics of English, important as they are. Grammar and usage bow to arbitrary rules that change over time. Elegance never goes out of style. His enthusiasm for language, for literature, for ideas, even for my woeful attempts at writing, opened a world of possibilities to me.

Other mentors, among them gifted teachers, later nudged me along my path. But his was the breath of inspiration that kindled my mind's banked fires. He planted the seeds: that ideas unleash the imagination; that words move us to good, to evil, to indifference; that the mind is worth exploring; that a wondrous world awaits.

To be Mr. Bott's student was a priceless gift, an awakening to the glory of knowledge and, thus, to a lifelong search for wisdom. ◆

# Mary June Burd

Mary June Burd lives in the state of Maryland, less than ten miles from the White House in our nation's capitol. She grew up in Chicago, where she met her Prince Charming: Laurence Burd, a reporter for the *Chicago Tribune*. Soon he was promoted to the *Tribune*'s Washington Bureau, becoming their White House correspondent. Mary June and Laurence "Bud," were married for forty-four wonderful years before he passed away. Mary June is the mother of four, "Nana Extraordinaire" to nine grandchildren, and hopes to have the joy of knowing at least one great-grandchild in her lifetime.

Over the years, Mary June has been involved with Planned Parenthood, church activities, fund-raising for Children's Hospital, and P.E.O.—a national women's organization dedicated to raising funds for women's higher education.

To quote her daughter Sally, "Mom is full of love and goodness, always brings a smile and a compliment to others, and those who meet her walk away with a chuckle, a quote or story to lighten their load. Whenever she is around, the world seems a better place."

MARY JANE BURD'S TEACHER WITH CLASS IS
❤ MRS. PRESTON

# Mrs. Preston

*I*t was the roaring '20s. Babe Ruth, Jack Dempsey, and Red Grange were becoming legends that live on today. So, too, Mrs. Preston, my third-grade teacher at Bryn E. Stolp Elementary School, lives on through her wisdom taught to her third-grade class.

Not very many women (or men) dyed their hair in those days, but Mrs. Preston did! There were no radios, TV, or video games, and movies were silent, so our greatest anticipation was what shade Mrs. Preston's hair would be each Monday morning. What else do you think about in Wilmette, Illinois, if you are eight years old?

Mrs. Preston was full of fascinating facts and wisdom, which were presented in a way eight-year-olds could comprehend and that would make us giggle as well. Mrs. Preston's wisdom was decades ahead of her time. Written at the top of the blackboard in beautiful Palmer Method cursive writing was Mrs. Preston's motto:

"Every day do your work,

You'll be glad you did not shirk."

Simple as it was, I lived by her motto. I think in some way, this helped me gain a full academic scholarship to Grinnel College in Iowa. After college, I remembered her advice throughout my years working with high school students and raising four children with my wonderful husband. Seventy-five years later, a current best-seller, *Sunscreen*, has an introduction with the same admonition:

"Do your work, you never know when routine life will delight and surprise you." *Mrs. Preston lives on!* ❦

*A teacher affects eternity;*
*he can never tell where*
*his influence stops.*

— **Henry Brooks Adams**

# Marian Wright Edelman

Marian Wright Edelman, founder and president of the Children's Defense Fund (CDF), has been an advocate for disadvantaged Americans her entire career. Under her leadership, the Washington-based CDF has become a strong national voice for children and families.

Mrs. Edelman, a graduate of Spelman College and Yale Law School, began her career in the mid 1960s. As the first black woman admitted to the Mississippi bar, she directed the NAACP Legal Defense and Educational Fund office in Jackson, Mississippi. In 1968, she moved to Washington, D.C., as counsel for the Poor People's March that Dr. Martin Luther King Jr. began organizing before his death. She also founded the Washington Research Project, a public-interest law firm and the parent body of the Children's Defense Fund. For two years she served as the director of the Center for Law and Education at Harvard University. In 1973, she began the CDF.

MARIAN WRIGHT EDELMAN'S TEACHER WITH CLASS IS
### PROFESSOR HOWARD ZINN

# Professor Howard Zinn

*I* grew up in Bennettsville, South Carolina, the daughter of a Baptist preacher. My parents had the most important influence on me while I was growing up and are responsible for the values I received as a child. I also fell under the influence of the community elders, who saw themselves as an essential part in the raising of the town's children. It was a role that was expected of them.

I went to Spelman College in Atlanta. It was a staid woman's college that developed safe, young women who married Moorehouse men, helped raise a family, and never kicked up dust.

My History professor there, Howard Zinn, taught me the value of questioning the status quo and illustrated the power inherent in an individual. Professor Zinn got us involved in the political climate of the times. This was the South of the late 1950s, where the first attempts at social and political change in the struggle for civil rights originated.

Professor Zinn would take us outside the sheltered stone wall of the Spelman gates to the realities of interracial dialogues and protests. The activism we initially took part in preceded the regional and national movements that are usually referred to as the civil rights era. One of our first actions was to protest the policy of public library segregation. Protesters (predominately college students) walked into the Carnegie Library in Atlanta asking librarians for such works as John Stuart Mill's *On Liberty* or John Locke's *An Essay Concerning Human Understanding*. Some asked for the U.S. Constitution and others for the Declaration of Independence. Using such tactics, the Atlanta Library Board changed its segregationist policy. It was actions such as these that led to further protests, further questioning, and striving for basic American freedoms. It was the beginning of a movement for many of us.

Professor Zinn was instrumental in helping me get a fellowship for a junior year abroad. He had a lot of faith in me as a young girl and felt that traveling on my own would benefit me more than going with the Smith or Sweetbriar groups.

I left the United States in 1958 and traveled through Europe for fifteen months. My year abroad gave me the confidence to take risks and follow my own path. It made me more of an individual; it gave me a sense of myself. It also exposed me to the possibilities of the world. There was so much out there, so much to see and experience. My year abroad was a very special time, it was a time of awakening.

I returned to Atlanta to find a more socially and racially tense city. Opinions had grown stronger on both sides, and the consequences of those opinions were taking shape in the worst of ways. Professor Zinn continued to involve students in civil rights issues and led them to more protests and rallies.

It was also at this time that I decided to go to law school. It was something I had never thought of before, but somewhere in the course of my travels it became a reality for me. I graduated from Spelman in 1960 and went to Yale Law School. After receiving my degree I returned to Mississippi to continue my activism with the Student Nonviolent Coordinating Committee, which organized most of the voter registrations and protests for blacks in the Deep South, many resulting in violent confrontations with small-town law officers and locals.

Professor Zinn responded to a yearning in the younger generation to make a difference, and like all good teachers, he brought out the best in people. He was concerned with justice, and everyone around him caught his concern. He was a very special man whose political activities eventually got him fired from Spelman. He went on to Boston University and became an outspoken critic of the Vietnam War.

Well into his seventies, Professor Zinn remains an optimist. He has been a prolific writer of numerous books, including the controversial *A People's History of the United States* and *You Can't Be Neutral on a Moving Train*. He doesn't teach anymore, but is a very busy public speaker. I am grateful to him for fostering in me the belief that I could make a difference; it is something I have carried with me ever since.

As I watched Andrew Young being sworn in as the mayor of Atlanta in 1981, I felt such a sense of accomplishment. Before the ceremony, I ate lunch in a cafeteria where I had protested and been arrested years before. I had come full circle. 🪶

# *Lisa Howorth*

Lisa Howorth taught art history and southern studies at the University of Mississippi for ten years. She has published two books: *The South: A Treasury of Art and Literature* and *Yellowdogs, Hushpuppies and Bluetick Hounds: The Official Encyclopedia of Southern Culture Quiz Book.* Currently, she is a literature panelist for the National Endowment for the Arts.

LISA HOWORTH'S TEACHER WITH CLASS IS
∾ **MRS. LECHLITER**

# Mrs. Lechliter

or some reason most high school English students read the short (it's not) story "The Bear" if they are required to read anything by William Faulkner. On the surface, "The Bear" is a fine example of regional literature—a hunting story set in the Deep South, rich with local color. Like much of Faulkner's writing, beneath the deceptive simplicity of the story is an incredibly complex Shakespearean tragedy, a tale that encapsulates the whole exalted and miserable history of the South and all its people. In other words, it is way over the heads of the average high school student. It was certainly way over mine. Although I was fascinated by Faulkner's language, exotic characters, and powerful landscape, the deep secrets and historical insights mostly eluded me. That was until the story was explicated by my excellent eleventh-grade English teacher, Elizabeth Lechliter.

There is one very dramatic yet subtle scene in "The Bear" when a young man reads over his grandfather's plantation ledgers, which reveal a dark and horrifying part of his family (and the South's) history.

I never would have gathered the full implications of this passage on my own. However, after Mrs. Lechliter illuminated it I was dumbstruck by Faulkner's compelling narrative.

Although I have always been a reader, the care taken by Mrs. Lechliter in teaching this story opened up literature in a new way for me. It was from that time on that I became absorbed with the amazing power of writers to create a world out of history, memory, experience, and passion, and to draw readers into it.

When I was about twenty or twenty-one, I could resist the pull of Faulkner's fictional Yoknapatawpha County no longer. I moved to the South where I have been ever since—a quarter of a century spent teaching, writing, editing, helping with my husband's bookstore, and meeting many of the writers who come to Oxford to give readings. I don't know if Mrs. Lechliter is still in this world, but I hope that she somehow knew that she *literally* changed my life. ❧

*It is the supreme art of the teacher to awaken joy in creative expression and knowledge.*

— **Albert Einstein**


*The human mind is our fundamental resource.*

— **John Fitzgerald Kennedy**

# Stephen F. Levinson, M.D., Ph.D.

Stephen F. Levinson grew up in Indianapolis and went on to obtain an M.D. from Indiana University and a Ph.D. in Electrical Engineering from Purdue University. Following residency training at Stanford, he was employed at the National Institutes of Health for a number of years, during which he had the opportunity to do research in Japan. He is currently chairman of the Department of Physical Medicine and Rehabilitation at the University of Rochester Medical Center. Dr. Levinson and his wife, Susan, have traveled all over the world. In his very limited free time, he enjoys photography, hiking, and reading.

STEPHEN LEVINSON'S TEACHER WITH CLASS IS
## ❦ MR. ERNEST MORRISON

# MR. ERNEST MORRISON

*M*r. Morrison was the most unlikely of heroes, but he is certainly one of mine. He grew up on a farm and always had a farm story to tell. I don't know why he chose to leave his rural roots to pursue a career in teaching, but one always had a sense that he remained a country boy at heart. I know that most of my classmates considered him to be a bit "out of it"—a country bumpkin who just loved math and loved teaching it.

When I first met Mr. Morrison, I was about to become a teenager and very unsure of myself in every possible way. It didn't help matters that my school record wasn't the greatest. I excelled in science, but little else. In fact, I was labeled a "slow reader." Because of the difficulties I had with my studies, I was tested. Ironically, I was found to be "gifted." One would never have guessed from my grades. The expert who tested me felt that my best hope was for my school to take a big gamble and place me in an accelerated program. They agreed. I was terribly nervous and of course feared failure. Classes were very difficult for me. Everyone in this program was getting A's and B's and I was struggling just to maintain a C average.

Mr. Morrison never gave up on me, however. Somehow, he saw that I had an unusual aptitude for math. He spent extra time with me and helped me understand fractions that were difficult for me to grasp without his help. He put everything into perspective and explained concepts in a way that made complete sense to me. He not only taught me math but gave me confidence and self-esteem. He was so patient, and yet allowed me to leap forward when I was ready. As I became more proficient in math, my skills began to improve in my other classes as well. By the end of seventh grade I had a solid A average—a record that I maintained throughout the rest of junior high, high school, college, and medical school.

Today, people seem to take it for granted that I am very bright, that everything comes easily to me. In 1968 it sure didn't seem that way. Had it not been for the patience and guidance of Mr. Morrison, I might never have developed the confidence to work hard and succeed as a physician and medical researcher. ❧

*I* touch the future.

*I teach.*

**— Christa McAuliffe**

*T*eaching should be
such that what is offered
is perceived as a valuable gift
and not as a hard duty.

**— Albert Einstein**

# Walter Cronkite

Walter Cronkite has covered virtually every major news event during his more than sixty years in journalism—the last forty-eight affiliated with CBS News. He became a special correspondent for CBS News on March 6, 1981, when he stepped down as anchorman and managing editor of the *CBS Evening News* after nearly nineteen years in that role.

A sampling of Cronkite's assignments for CBS News over three decades reads like a synopsis of American and world history—exclusive interviews with most major heads of state, including all U.S. presidents since Harry S. Truman; all aspects of the American political scene since 1952, including Watergate; and news-making events around the world, including the Vietnam War and the siege of the American Embassy in Iran. Cronkite's unflappability under pressure inspired the affectionate nickname of "Old Iron Pants," while his accomplishments earned him acclaim from his journalism colleagues, other professionals, and the American public.

WALTER CRONKITE'S TEACHER WITH CLASS IS
❦ **MR. FRED BIRNEY**

# Mr. Fred Birney

*I* went to San Jacinto High School in Houston, Texas, in the 1930s and was fortunate to come in contact with a man who would inspire me to become a career print and broadcast journalist. Fred Birney was a pioneer in high school journalism. Very few high schools at that time even taught journalism, and many schools didn't have their own student newspaper.

Fred talked the Houston Board of Education into allowing him to teach a journalism class once a week at three local high schools, one of which was San Jacinto. He was a newspaperman of the old school and taught us a great deal about reporting and writing. He also became a sponsor of the San Jacinto High School newspaper, the *Campus Cub*. Under his tutelage, we published it monthly, whereas it had previously been published in a casual manner just three or four times a year. During my junior year, I was the sports editor of the *Campus Cub* and its chief editor in my senior year.

Fred was a hands-on technical teacher, explaining the complexities of layout and copy. He also stressed the importance of the tight lead—the diminished inverted pyramid of an article's development and the necessity of taking an honest approach toward the subject matter.

At the time, I was an avid reader of *American Boy Magazine*, which was composed of a series of short stories to inspire boys to follow certain careers. I remember reading an article about mining engineers. I wish I had read an article about petroleum engineering in Texas in the 1930s instead of becoming interested in mineral mining. So here I was about to graduate, and I was torn between becoming a mining engineer and a journalist. Things could have been a lot different for me without Fred.

He was well-connected with the three newspapers in Houston. During the summer of my junior year, he secured his interested students jobs as copy boys and girls with the *Houston Post*. Then, after I graduated in 1933, I became the campus correspondent for the *Houston Post* at the University of Texas at Austin and worked at the college paper, the *Daily Texan*, working my way up to become its editor. My sophomore year I got a weekend job working as an exalted copy boy for the International News Service at the state capitol, but I was also asked to cover committee meetings of the state legislature.

That same year I was hired as a full-time cub reporter with the Scripps Howard Bureau, where I was taken under the wing of another newsman, Vann Kennedy. He gave me a great deal of advice and tutelage, and many chances to cover stories at the capitol.

Texas politics was an interesting arena for a budding journalist because the state legislative committee meetings addressed a number of special interest areas: farming, timber, cotton, mining, and many others. All these groups lobbied the various politicians to advance their own legislative self-interest.

At this time the country was in a time of immense transition. Technology was advancing at a rapid rate, and the money generated by these special interest groups, especially in Texas, was growing rapidly. It was an exciting time to be covering politics at any level.

At the end of my sophomore year, I was offered a job as a full-time reporter at the *Houston Press*. Roy Roussel was the city editor and his brother Peter was the culture editor. They helped me a great deal and I learned a lot from them. I was with the *Press* for a year and a half and never returned to college.

I was visiting my grandparents in Kansas City in 1936 when I saw an ad in the *Kansas City Star* for a job at a radio station, broadcasting football games in Oklahoma. Radio was new at the time and it was an exciting opportunity; it was in its primitive stages then—we got the news straight off the wire service. So I applied for the job and was hired to cover University of Oklahoma football games and news for WKY in Oklahoma City. However, the job lacked the excitement of my previous reporting experience.

I covered football until the threat of war became more of a reality. It was then that I realized my need to get back into news reporting. I was hired by the United Press, where I stayed for eleven years and served as a war correspondent during World War II. In 1950 I was hired by CBS and became further involved in radio and television.

Fred Birney wouldn't admire the type of journalism going on today. He was always big on journalistic integrity. "You've got to remember that everyone you write about is a human being," he would tell us, "not just a headline."

We exchanged several letters until his death, shortly after my high school graduation. He taught me so much in those high school classes, and by securing me those early jobs, he cemented my desire to be a reporter for the rest of my life. He was my major inspiration. I always credit Fred Birney for my career. ☙

*In the fifth grade, I was in a predominantly white school. Growing up with a white mother, I didn't have a woman of color to relate to. My teacher, Ms. Sims, was a woman like me, a woman of color. I thought, I can grow up to be like her.*

**— Halle Berry**

# Charles Henry Bohl

Charles (Chip) Bohl grew up in Urbana, Ohio. He is an architect, splitting his time between Annapolis, Maryland, and Los Angeles, California. In his architectural practice he views each project as an opportunity for his client to be a graduate student in their own special architectural program. The work of Bohl Architects has been featured nationally in newspapers, magazines, and television, and has been awarded recognition from the American Institute of Architects and the National Park Service. He enjoys history and architectural theory, and dreams of sculpting stone in Pietrasanta, Italy.

CHIP BOHL'S TEACHER WITH CLASS IS
## ✇ MR. WARE

# MR. WARE

*M*r. Ware was a young black man in an old white woman's domain. Most of my previous grammar school teachers were spinsters partial to librarian shoes, calf-length print dresses, and hair buns. Mr. Ware was the only male teacher in South Ward Elementary; the only other adult men were the head principal and the custodian. The fact that he was black was of little consequence. Our school had less than two hundred kids in six grades, and was about half white. The custodian, Mr. Roberts, was black, gentle, and kind. He kept a couple of small chairs in the closet under the stairs with the cleaning supplies, brooms, and mops, where he would eat his lunch with his granddaughter Roberta, who was in our class.

In 1961, Mr. Ware taught fifteen of us in the sixth grade. He was an athletic, muscular, handsome man. He spoke in a deep and rich voice with perfect diction, except when he took on a character in one of his many spontaneous theatrical presentations. When math became tedious and some kids nodded off, Mr. Ware would spin around from the blackboard, pull a poem from his desk, and read it full volume with great animation and vibrato. He was partial to Elizabethan presentations of J. Ogden Nash.

The sixth grade was a make or break point for many of us. The play and humor of grade school was being replaced with serious hard study for "your future." Some of us could see a future, but some were so handicapped by family neglect that time would only bring another tomorrow just like today.

Dwight was one of the lost kids. Sometimes we would not see him for days. He would come to school dirty, wearing the same clothes for weeks. He never did homework, did not carry books, and had no overcoat. He always sat in the back corner of the room.

At the end of the year, we had the big science project. Each student was assigned an individual project. Mr. Ware carefully created and assigned the projects to us based on one's skill and capacity for challenge. The day he announced the assignment of each science project was filled with apprehension and fear. His presentation of the assignments was dramatic and theatrical. He stood at the front of the class and formally read each student's full name, the assignment, and a brief description of the discovery, testing, and hypothesis of the scientific method. He assigned the easiest projects first. So the sooner your name was announced, the less difficult your assignment. As he neared the end, there was a long pause. Dwight was the last assigned.

Dwight was getting the most difficult project! Mr. Ware, at the peak of his presentation, taking on the postures of both preacher and three ring circus announcer, declared that Dwight was going to show the class the principles of the "chain reaction"! Chain reaction! That was for real scientists, and physicists and top secret formulas for the "A" bomb and the "H" bomb. We were all in shock; we all turned to look at Dwight, who was also in shock.

In the next days and weeks we were busy with our science projects. Mr. Ware worked with us individually at our desks to discuss our progress and problems. Inspired by his energy and attention, we were all keyed to produce our best possible project.

Dwight's project was somewhat shrouded in mystery. Mr. Ware would talk with him at his desk in hushed tones. Dwight would get upset, and slump. Then he would get back up again and work. It was not clear if he would make it.

The big day of the science project presentations was filled with both anxiety and relief. The most difficult projects involving chemistry and physics were building in complexity. Mr. Ware introduced the last one: Dwight's "chain reaction" project on the display table at the side of the room. Dwight approached the table and positioned a long board on top of two bricks. He lit a kitchen match at one end of the board, and a sequential eruption of flames raced across the board. Everyone was shocked as a blue smoke cloud grew up out of the board and drifted across the room. Dwight had cut the ends off kitchen matches, and glued the heads beside each other in a line to illustrate the principle of the chain reaction. We all cheered at the culmination of the science projects. Mr. Ware stood at the front of the room with his arms crossed over his chest, and a huge proud smile on his face. Dwight stood square and beamed at Mr. Ware. It seemed like their eyes were locked forever.

I learned so much from Mr. Ware by watching how he taught Dwight. ✺

# Chris Lord

Chris Lord was born in Bridgeport, Connecticut, and is the oldest of six children. His entire family moved to a small town in Iowa when he was five years old to join an Indian holy man and study Transcendental Meditation. After fourteen years he left the corn, soy beans, and occasional skateboarding adventures behind and hustled off to the University of Iowa. After a freshman year that can only be described as "dull," he followed his recently relocated family to Boulder, Colorado. He enrolled at the University of Colorado, where he quickly set about to earn a B.A. in creative writing.

He is known for his creativity, multiple ear piercings, and great relationships with the students. When he's not racing around the local roads or trails on his bike, he is off backpacking the Appalachian trail, reading from an intimidating stack of books, sitting through classic and poor films alike, or spending time with his wife, Erin, a middle- and upper-school music teacher, and their daughter, Finley Blue.

Chris teaches seventh-grade civics, history, and English as well as coaching soccer and helping to run the outdoor program at his school.

CHRIS LORD'S TEACHER WITH CLASS IS
🍎 **MR. BROZ**

# MR. BROZ

*G*rowing up in a small town in the Midwest I was accustomed to the nature of the local folk. I was considered a rebel of sorts, as a member of a group of skateboarding troublemakers who, to say the least, were not the most favored kids in town.

But in my spare time I discovered my love for poetry. I would spend a good deal of my free time (both in and out of class) filling ragged spiral notebooks with words expressing my own thoughts. As my school did not have any poetry classes and basic English did not provide poetry as an option, I spent many chemistry, algebra, and computer classes scribbling in my notebook.

In tenth grade, I was lucky to grab a space in Mr. Broz's class. It was there that I discovered that a "hip" beatnik of a teacher, complete with a goatee, turtleneck, and patches on his sport coat, lived in our midst.

The main focus of the class was writing formal essays. However, Mr. Broz was very pleased with my work and soon challenged me with controversial political issues and current events, forcing me to examine my own beliefs and values. When my ten-page paper on the crimes in South Africa was lost in the hard drive by what I believe was the *original* computer virus, he allowed me to sit and evaluate the topic orally.

Soon he discovered my love for poetry and allowed me to complete my assignments using poems in place of essays. On top of that, Mr. Broz discovered weekend poetry workshops at colleges and paid my tuition. He was always eager to read my newest writing and constantly encouraged me to search for my own voice. He exposed me to other poets and writers and prodded me when I needed to excel.

Mr. Broz inspired me to pursue something that I loved and enriched my abilities. He truly cared about me, taught me to learn, and helped me discover that my voice was crucial. For this I will always be grateful. ❦

*The useful type of successful teacher is the one whose main interest is the children, not the subject.*

**— Sir Walter Raleigh**

*When I am forgotten,
as I shall be,
And sleep in dull cold marble,
Say I taught thee.*

**— William Shakespeare, Henry VIII, Act III, Sc. 2**

# Elaine Conklin Shreve

Elaine Conklin Shreve attended Good Samaritan School of Nursing in Portland, Oregon, where she still resides. Mrs. Shreve has been married to Donald Shreve for thirty-five years. The couple has four sons. Shreve retired from nursing in 1992 as Beaverton, Oregon, School District Head of Health Services.

ELAINE CONKLIN SHREVE'S TEACHER WITH CLASS IS
## MRS. MABEL FROST

# Mrs. Mabel Frost

We are experiencing great challenges in education with concepts such as "inclusion" and "ungraded primaries" and team teaching. To a little girl growing up in the 1930s and '40s, these concepts were real experiences at Cairo School. My two brothers, sister, and I attended a two-room school about ten miles outside of Ontario, a small Oregon town on the Idaho border. As children in a poor struggling farm family during the Great Depression, beset with an alcoholic and ill parent, we found our teachers were the single greatest influence outside of our home.

Mrs. Frost was the teacher in the "big room" and Mrs. Peck the teacher in the "little room" with four lower grades. They both were beacons of education and stability in this rural community. My clearest memories are of Mrs. Frost, a tall, slender, plain woman with "coiffed" hair who wore brightly colored two-piece wool suits while most of our mothers wore simple house dresses or farm work clothes. When Physical Education was first required in the 1940s, she trooped us out by the girls' outhouse and led us in exercises in her two-piece suit.

The desks in the big room were lined up by grade in four rows. The fifth grade was over by the windows, the sixth next. The seventh grade row was short because the stove sat at the back of that row. Then the eighth grade was over by the wall of the little room. A large picture of George Washington hung in the front of the room. The ledge by the window held several bottles wrapped with twine.

These were filled with cattails we had colored in a spiral design with crayons.

We had all sorts of kids, about twenty-five in each room. My brother was the only student in fifth grade so he was put into sixth grade. The migrant children came in about March each year. Many Japanese families from the internment camps relocated there in order to provide labor in the fields. Their children often didn't speak English. A friend's large family lived year-round in a tent with wooden sides. So our modest one-bedroom house without a sink or bathroom didn't seem unusual. We saw that our teachers found special importance in each child no matter what his/her age or background.

We liked to have everyone go to the blackboards that lined three walls to practice math or diagram sentences together. They instilled in us the understanding that you were to help your neighbor. We were allowed to take spelling or other tests that an upper grade was taking as long as our other work was done. Older students frequently monitored a younger reading group or provided individual assistance.

Mrs. Frost taught penmanship with "arm movement" and our decorated penmanship books were filled with pages of carefully written ovals and "up and downs." After I sent my first "business letter" to Carlsbad Caverns, I received brochures that showed a world beyond my imagination. What power to be able to get such information! I also wrote for information about Norway when we each selected a country to study. My project book contained exciting pictures and stories about fjords, glaciers, and reindeer. The book *Snow Treasure* still brings tears to my eyes.

Sometimes we learned about things for the future. The word "vacation" was introduced as a spelling word, however the concept was beyond our understanding. The word had no relation to our dairy farm where cows needed to be milked twice every day. My brothers and I talked about the word several years later when we discovered someone who had actually taken a vacation. We also learned about traffic lights and memorized what the red, green, and yellow meant, which we'd surely need to know if we ever went to New York City.

Most of our lessons were relevant to our daily lives. I was excited to learn about the Oregon Trail because it was located only a few miles away from our school. We created project books detailing pioneer life. We could easily understand the life of the pioneer with his wagons and horses; it was much like our own. I cut out a map of the Oregon Trail from the newspaper and pasted it on my project book cover, which I shaped like Oregon. The blue paper at the far edge represented the ocean that we'd never seen. The eastern side of Oregon was a crooked line following the Snake River, which we did cross frequently. Books such as Laura Ingalls Wilder's helped to stoke a romantic view of the frontier world.

One of my favorite times was after lunch when Mrs. Frost would read to us. She read such classics as *Wind in the Willows* but our favorites were Nancy Drew. Sometimes we just couldn't stand to have her stop and would promise all sorts of good behavior if she'd just read one more chapter. She confessed that she hoped the County School Superintendent would not make a visitation and find her reading Nancy Drew to us!

Our school musicals and plays were presented twice a year. My mother often had to create four to six costumes for us, from trees to rabbits to sailor suits. The plays were presented at the local Grange Hall and were the social highlights of the community. Mrs. Frost found the roles that best suited each child. A very shy Japanese boy had a lovely voice and we were all pleased when she got him to sing a solo.

Sometimes Mrs. Frost organized a box lunch or pie social before the plays to raise money for schoolbooks. The women and girls decorated their boxes with crepe paper and whisked them secretly to the display table so their identity wasn't known. Then the auctioneer began the bidding by the men and boys. Of course, the real competition was between the women to provide the most delicious pie. Our eighth-grade graduation service at the Grange Hall was attended by the community. This had been preceded by our traditional surprise skip-day. The five students in eighth grade packed our lunches and met early that day for a ten- to fifteen-mile bike ride to the local landmark, Malheur Butte. After climbing to the top of the butte, we then went home with the delicious sense of having skipped school, something that responsible farm kids just didn't do. For our graduation, Mr. and Mrs. Frost took all five of us out to dinner at the Country Club, a place famous for its fried chicken. Mrs. Frost taught us to put the cloth napkins in our laps and to wipe our mouths after each bite of chicken. This was a very special occasion to go to a restaurant, especially without our parents.

Mr. Frost repaired most things around the school. He also drove Mrs. Frost out to school when the snow was really deep and would start the fire in the coal stoves at the back of each room. My observations of their cordial relationship and her occasional comments about their home life were an important vision of a home far different from my own.

As today's teachers search for more effective classroom techniques, many are rediscovering the legacy of skills and dedication that teachers used to meet the needs of students in a variety of settings. This legacy includes multiage rooms, ungraded primaries, team teaching, collaborative learning, theme units, and portfolio assessment. My portfolio is in a box in my basement. It is filled with grateful memories of our teacher who guided and inspired the children who are today's leaders, workers, and parents.

Thank you, Mrs. Frost, and all those teachers who touch children's lives. What you do and say every day is important to tomorrow's leaders and families. ❧

# Cindy Crawford

Having appeared on over four hundred magazine covers throughout the United States and Europe, Cindy Crawford is one of the most recognizable faces in the world. She has numerous film and television credits and is the author of Cindy Crawford's *Basic Face*, a makeup workbook, and *About Face*, a photo book of children.

Cindy made a smooth transition from the world of fashion and beauty into the arena of broadcast journalism as host of MTV's *House of Style*, which she hosted for six years. Cindy is also an acclaimed producer.

Among Cindy's many other credits are *Fair Game*, a feature film in which she starred opposite William Baldwin; *Muppets Tonight*, which she guest-hosted; and numerous specials for Fox-TV.

Born and raised in DeKalb, Illinois, she has become one of the most successful models of all time. She is the spokesperson for *Strength for Caring*, a national education and support program for cancer caregivers, and she donates a great deal of time and energy to the Leukemia Society of America, in memory of her brother, who died at age three from the blood disorder.

Cindy commutes between New York and Los Angeles. She is married to Rande Gerber and they have two children.

CINDY CRAWFORD'S TEACHER WITH CLASS IS
## ∼ MR. HALVORSON

# MR. HALVORSON

*I* have been blessed throughout my life by encountering people who have enabled me to grow and develop as an individual.

I was fortunate to have great teachers every year in school. In the fourth grade I had a student teacher determined to confer nicknames on her students. I was dubbed "Future Miss America." She helped me to understand that beyond the confines of my hometown there was a whole world of possibilities to explore.

Mr. Halvorson, my high school calculus teacher, was an exceptional person. I appreciated the fact that he was both an authority figure and a friend. He emphasized that the world is a bigger place than our familiar neighborhood. He filled his students with excitement and anticipation for the future. Mr. Halvorson also taught me a strong lesson—that learning can be fun.

I have been fortunate to know extraordinary individuals who have consistently been strong influences on my life. They have challenged me and empowered me to develop my talents and become successful. I cannot remember a year when I did not have their sage counsel and encouragement when needed. Mr. Halvorson is among the many wonderful people who have enabled me to be who I am today. ❧

# Keith R. Benson, Ph.D.

Keith R. Benson is the program director at the National Science Foundation in charge of history, philosophy, and sociology of science.

He was professor of the history of biology in the Program for the History of Science, Technology, and Medicine at the University of Washington. He also held positions in the history and philosophy departments as well as serving on the faculty at Oregon State University and University of California, San Diego. He has taught courses that include the history of the life sciences, and written extensively on American biology, particularly examining its early beginnings at Johns Hopkins University. He is coeditor of *The Development of American Biology* and *The American Expansion of Biology*, and recently edited the translation of Jacques Roger's classic book, *The Life Sciences in Eighteenth-century France.* He is also the coeditor of a soon-to-be released work on the history of modern oceanography. Dr. Benson recently completed a six-year term as executive secretary of the History of Science Society and is currently treasurer of the International Society of the History, Philosophy, and Social Studies of Biology.

In addition to enjoying an active speaking schedule and consulting practice that has taken him around the world, Keith makes his primary home on Vashon Island in Puget Sound, Washington. He divides his time between his hand-built treehome and a boat he recently refurbished, once owned by former president Herbert Hoover.

KEITH BENSON'S TEACHERS WITH CLASS ARE
§ PROFESSORS DUVALL, FARBER, AND WILLIAMS

# Professor R. Fenton Duvall
# Professor Paul Lawrence Farber
# Professor Williams

When I first decided to attend graduate school in 1970, two motives spurred me on. First, the prospect of a nine-to-five job had less than minimal appeal. Second, although a recent college graduate, my experience in higher education had only indicated how little I knew, not how educated I was. Certainly, to describe myself as a finished and educated individual would stretch the veracity and credibility of the word "educated."

Despite my educational insecurity, I had a wonderful experience as an undergraduate, especially when I listened attentively to the lectures of R. Fenton Duvall, an economic historian from the University of Pennsylvania. He was the first to expose me to the economic motives of the nineteenth-century American expansion to the west, the power of primary source materials such as those that described the brutal treatment of native Americans, and taught me the value of learning to "wrestle intellectually" with ideas, concepts, and abstractions. Duvall was soft-spoken, congenial, and exceptionally well-organized, and I soon found myself emulating his style. I even decided there was merit in eating an entire apple, including the core, simply because Professor Duvall ate his apple in this manner. The mystery behind his use of the letter "R" in place of his first name introduced me to historical research. Although locating his full first name in an academic directory was not very difficult, it was my first successful venture in the library, and from that point I was hooked.

Professor Duvall's comment on one of my papers, "Good, but not much mental perspiration here," not only created a desire in me to work harder for him but it also served to illustrate just how much work the academic life demanded. There was always more to do, something more to consider. Equipped with this attitude, I entered graduate school in 1971 at Oregon State University, where I almost immediately found myself drawn to Professor Paul Lawrence Farber. Nattily attired, erudite, extremely well-read, and the epitome of sophistication, Professor Farber seemed to be light-years ahead of me and the perfect model to mold my own academic career upon. The only problem was that he found me to be his antithesis. Thus, when I informed him of my desire to work with him, he told me of his personal reservations. After a lengthy conversation in which he expanded upon Professor Duvall's notion of perspiring with the mind, he reluctantly agreed to serve as my Master's degree mentor. I knew from this point that my notion of hard work would have to be raised to another quantum level.

Everything about Professor Farber was inspiring. I never attended one lecture in which I was not stimulated; new ideas, new books, new historical figures all became alive and exciting for me. Literature, music, art, philosophy, history, science, and politics became the grist for his lecture mill, producing fascinating interpretations of eighteenth-century natural history, nineteenth-century evolution theory, and twentieth-century genetics. By my second year at Oregon State, he seemed to note that I had some promise and soon he and his wonderful wife Vreneli Farber, a scholar of Russian literature and cinema, began to invite me to their home for social occasions. Surrounded by walls filled with art, classical music in the background, and food that was exceptional, I found myself completely captivated and all my senses completely sated.

Despite my growing maturity as a scholar, I was still aware of my limitations. Professor Farber and I had weekly conversations, which often included nonacademic matters, but I could still not convince myself that he had accepted me as a young colleague. Even the weekly dinner invitations that were sent were not sufficient to allow me the luxury of regarding Professor Farber as a personal friend. But to this very day, I remember the long stroll we took from campus to his home after the successful defense of my dissertation. He reached into his pocket, extracted a cigar, and offered his hand to me stating, "That was the best defense I have ever witnessed." My sense of exhilaration was unbelievable. Hearing a revered mentor describe my performance in this manner made me realize that maybe, just maybe, I was becoming intellectually sophisticated.

Professor Farber has always remained my role model. Shortly after my education was completed at Oregon State, he was named as one of the first "University Professors" at the school, and honored for his teaching. His mentoring of graduate students continues today. Additionally, I am grateful to Professor Farber for his suggestion that I ask Professor William Appleman Williams to become a member of my dissertation committee. Professor Williams had established his academic career at the University of Wisconsin, where he was known locally and nationally as one of this country's leading Marxist historians. But the Vietnam War and its protests had thoroughly disillusioned him, so he moved to his beloved Oregon coast home, and began to teach in the University's history department with the understanding that he would not be asked to have any committee assignments, including the advising of graduate students (Oregon State lacked any graduate program in history at the time, so this was not a large concession on the part of the University). I am not sure Professor Farber knew of this agreement, but I was certainly unaware of it. Thus, Professor Williams was probably so surprised by my request (I had taken one course from him) that he forgot his lack of commitments when he responded affirmatively.

Maybe it was due to the influence of Professor Williams, but I soon found myself interested in discovering what Marxist historiography was all about. During one of my office visits, I asked him to advise me on reading in the area and he told me he would send along a reading list. To my astonishment, the reading list came shortly afterward, with a two-page letter appended (2 March 1977). The letter remains in my files and I occasionally refer to it for inspiration. Following his discussion of the difficulty of deciding what Marx thought about historical research, he concluded the letter with the following paragraph:

*I know that [his previous remarks] may sound more than a bit flippant, but none-the less [sic] I am serious about it all. There is always a choice about the **kind** of activism that is most consequential. If I had been in Cuba in 1958, then I would have been a great point man in an infantry squad. But right now the issue is to be the best intellectual making the best sense out of this **truly terrible** society.*

*So, **do it!***

*Much regard — Bill*

One might read Williams's thoughts and conclude that at the end of his career he had become so jaundiced about American society that he adopted a negative and cynical position. But this was not his position nor was it mine after reading his letter. While I cannot know his exact meaning with any precision, I am relatively certain his comments represented his reflection on the absurdity of life and the tragic consequences for so many people. For the intellectual, however, Williams considered a more optimistic mien; he or she was allowed to study the conditions behind the historical events and then attempt to interpret them. Again, I found these comments to be inspiring.

In looking back upon my undergraduate and graduate experiences, I feel so grateful that these three wonderful men came to occupy such meaningful roles in my life. I am not sure that any one of these individuals was aware of his influence upon me or even intended to exert any influence upon me. But I do know that my lifelong commitment to learning and my unquenchable thirst for knowledge was directly related to the example each of these individuals provided for me. As I face classes and as I discuss life and its meaning with students in my office, I am constantly reminded of the importance of learning and of carrying on the tradition I have inherited from them. ॐ

*Mrs. Bogard, my third- and fourth-grade teacher, read to us a lot post-lunchtime, and that was always the sleepy, hot part of the day. I remember getting really alert and excited when she'd read. Somehow it became my job to give her a wink if she stumbled or messed up—I don't know why. She gave me my love of reading.*

**— Actress Ashley Judd**

# Ross C. "Rocky" Anderson

**Mayor of Salt Lake City**

Mayor Anderson serves the office of mayor with energy and enthusiasm. Before serving as mayor he was an attorney specializing in a variety of civil litigation for twenty-one years, and has a long history of professional distinction, community activism, and volunteer experience.

Mayor Anderson, the proud father of a nineteen-year-old son, believes his greatest responsibility is to help make Salt Lake City a safe, healthy, vibrant city in which people of all ages, races, ethnic origins, religions, sexual orientations, and genders become active, equal, and welcomed participants in community life.

MAYOR ROSS ANDERSON'S TEACHER WITH CLASS IS
### ℰ MR. VOGEL

# MR. VOGEL

*M*r. Vogel, my sixth-grade teacher, was a combination of an extremely effective academic educator and a model of what it takes to be a compassionate, humorous, terrific human being. From activities like the daily multiplication-table drills, and our required participation in a science fair, to rather intense reading requirements, Mr. Vogel's class—all of us—learned what we should have, and more, in the sixth grade.

Mr. Vogel never allowed us to slack off and demanded that each of us do our academic best. But the aspect of Mr. Vogel that made him a lifetime inspiration was his kindness, warm humor, and his extraordinary efforts on behalf of each student.

I had recently moved with my family from Salt Lake City to Ogden, Utah, and did not know anyone except a cousin at my new school, Polk Elementary. I was apprehensive and not at all happy about the move to a new school. However, I learned Mr. Vogel was going to be my teacher, and my parents were told by neighbors that I had been assigned to a tremendous teacher whom everyone seemed to love. I discovered why right away.

Mr. Vogel knew I was the new kid in town and made certain I got to know the other students immediately. He seemed to take a personal interest in each of us, and if he perceived that any of us were having a particular problem, he attended to it sensitively and compassionately. We all knew that Mr. Vogel really cared about each of us.

I was out of school for an extended time with a medical problem. Mr. Vogel visited me at home and called my parents often to see how I was doing and provided me with my lessons so I would not fall too far behind. Later in the year, I injured my knee and had a cast on my leg for three months. Mr. Vogel helped me learn how to maneuver the stairs and often hung out with me during recess if I did not feel like hobbling outside to watch the other kids play.

The kids in Mr. Vogel's class learned the Golden Rule, not from being told about it, but by seeing it demonstrated daily by our teacher. Mr. Vogel was always genuinely kind and considerate toward his students. After a rash of thefts from students' desks and from the coat rack—everything from lunch tickets to a radio one student had brought from home—Mr. Vogel discovered that the thief was a boy who came from a wealthy Ogden family. When the boy was away from class, Mr. Vogel explained to us that the student was experiencing serious problems and that he needed our help and friendship. As a result of Mr. Vogel's discussion with us, we all learned a great lesson in empathy. No one ever said an unkind word to the boy, and we went out of our way to be friendlier to him. As a result of the understanding elicited from us by Mr. Vogel, a classroom of sixth-graders was transformed from a bunch of kids who had been angry about the thefts to a group of impressionable students who were truly concerned for the welfare of the boy who had stolen their things.

Mr. Vogel demonstrated to his students the joy and rewards that come from doing more than expected. Although it was not part of his teaching assignment,

Mr. Vogel taught many of us tumbling after school. The physical discipline he taught was something entirely new to most of us, and we loved it. As he pushed himself in going far beyond the call of duty by teaching us tumbling, so too did we learn to push ourselves in executing various tumbling maneuvers. We learned that discipline and hard work are good things and that, in the end, they bring about much happiness.

Mr. Vogel had high expectations of us, and we were happy and willing to work to meet them. Mr. Vogel was a man who was completely engaged in his teaching, and whose joy in his job was reflected in his good-natured smile and frequent laugh. Mr. Vogel clearly loved his job because he loved the people with whom he dealt every day—his students.

As with most of those who have positively impacted our lives, Mr. Vogel probably was not often told by his students or our parents what a tremendous teacher he was. But Mr. Vogel's obvious joy in his job reflected his knowledge that he was loved and admired by his students. Nevertheless, I would be very pleased to have the opportunity to say to Mr. Vogel, "Thank you so much for all you did for all your students. We've all had better, more enriched lives as a result. You were everything a good teacher should be!" 🐚

# *Winston Beigel*

**Winston Beigel is the son of a piano teacher and a freelance photographer. A graduate of Marymount Manhattan College with a B.A. in Communication Arts, Winston is now based out of New York City where he works as a private tutor while pursuing a career in screenplay writing. Winston has directed his own "Camp Comedy," where he shared his love of humor with young adults, and has made his television dreams a reality with internships at NBC's *Saturday Night Live* and *The Daily Show*. He recently completed his first full-length feature script, *Accidental Genius*, which is now being shopped to Hollywood and independent film producers.**

WINSTON BEIGEL'S TEACHER WITH CLASS IS
### 🎔 MS. JAYNE KARSTEN

# Ms. Jayne Karsten

*J*ayne Karsten may not know it, but she already is immortal. She is alive in circles larger than the desks that cluttered her classroom.

I was a bold-faced and impudent contraband of a student when I first walked into her classroom in my junior year of high school. I was humbled when Mrs. Karsten spoke of men like Eliot and Miller, Dante, Raskolnikov, and Shelley. She brought to life women like Dickinson, Austen, Anna Karenina, and Sister Carrie. She poured out their words like appealing beverages. She exposed them like layers of artichokes. These books she showed us were the hidden fruits of one thousand truths, each of them from the human experience, and inconceivably rich in beauty and meaning.

Never mind that this woman had already lived beyond the dreaming boundaries of these books. She had been an original cast member of the *Little Rascals*, choreographed with Duke Ellington, was a mother, a scholar, a former resident of Egypt. The truly dignified, wonderful Jayne Karsten had lived a life that had gone beyond normal expectations. She had done so voluntarily, with heart, imagination, zest, and energy. She rarely uttered a word about her personal conquests. You would have to pry. You just got the feeling that she was grateful to be there, sharing what she loved—life. And Jayne Karsten didn't just speak of written characters. She spoke of eras and times she'd lived through and experienced firsthand. She taught me how to waltz and dance the jitterbug. I sang Sinatra, did vaudeville, and learned the Crawdad song. And I was a student of the late nineties! Mrs. Karsten made history breathe and swing and rage with a fiery pulse. She came in dancing. I, like so many others, left her classroom with a spirit overflowing with her words and songs. She is immortal in a thousand hearts. ❧

*The world talks to the mind.
A teacher speaks more intimately;
he talks to the heart.*

— **Haim Ginott**

*I always tell students that
it is what you learn after
you know it all that counts.*

— **Harry S. Truman**

# *Marcella Yedid*

Marcella Yedid was born in Salonika, Greece, and immigrated to the United States with her family in 1956. With degrees from Indiana University's School of Music and from Brown University's graduate program in modern languages, she followed in her family's footsteps by becoming a French teacher in a small independent school in Cleveland, Ohio. For the last three decades, she has served as teacher and administrator in several independent schools in Ohio and Maryland. She is currently head of the Key School in Annapolis, Maryland.

Beyond her passion for teaching and interest in young people's development, she is an opera aficionado, active follower of international politics, and frequent traveler. A believer in the transformative capacity of the educational experience, she attributes her own achievements to the influences of a multitude of extraordinary teachers.

MARCELLA YEDID'S TEACHERS WITH CLASS ARE
 ❧ **MISS POSTANCE AND MR. POZA**

# MISS POSTANCE
# MR. POZA

*I*n identifying a teacher of consequence from the past, one who inspired, motivated, modeled, I found that we are all products of the multitudes who touch us at various junctures in our formative years. Each brings to bear a different icon of greatness. Two such teachers in particular come to mind.

At ten this image came to life for me in the form of the benign, smiling, blue-eyed countenance of a middle-aged woman named Miss Postance. Celibate yet mother to a class of fourth-graders, she exuded the loving nurturing for which a tentative, non-English-speaking, recently immigrated child was looking. Patient in her approach and embracing in her demeanor, Miss Postance's instruction went beyond the rudiments of reading, writing and arithmetic. She taught us about gentleness, sensitivity, and most of all humanity. Indeed, Miss Postance, the quintessential school marm from whom I learned the ethic of care and empathy, shall forever be the communicator of lessons transportable through life.

A decade later the icon of greatness was recast in the image of a dashing Mr. Roza, graduate assistant par excellence guiding a college freshman through a well-selected syllabus of French chef d'oeuvres. With an olive-toned Mediterranean visage, chestnut fiery eyes and complementary, short wavy hair, he exuded cosmopolitan flair and intellectual rigor. Well read and highly articulate, he came to class prepared to mesmerize us with his knowledge of poetry, criticism, and cultural trends. Passionately, he pursued ideas that nourished a young mind: existentialist thought and its impact on postwar Europe; idealism and pragmatism as seen through Anouilh's lens; feminism's rise as explicated by Steinem's giant precursor, Simone de Beauvoir. With his charm, intellectual prowess and engaging ideas he prompted fledgling scholars to adopt essential habits of mind: curiosity, critical thinking, disciplined analysis, and the penchant for the cerebral.

Which of these anchorings bears the greater consequence? An unworthy competition, for unquestionably the answer lies in both. The vulnerable young child needed Miss Postance's nurturing while the emerging adult succumbed to Mr. Roza's brilliance.

I am imprinted for life by two seemingly unlike individuals, who, on the surface, appear more disparate than may really be the case. In retrospect, I now surmise they both possessed a similar drive for effective teaching and a common flair for communicating who they really were. The qualities that each brought to bear on my impressionable young psyche, I now remember in distinct categories. But it is their highly homogenized blend that has extended its impact throughout my adult existence. ❧

*If* we forgot our homework,
came late to class or left our books
out on the desk, Mrs. Talbot, my
fourth-grade teacher, held us responsible
for what we did. That's crucial to learn
as a kid. . . . She made me feel special—
like I was somebody who mattered.
Today, she still comes to my concerts.

**— Country singer Jo Dee Messina**

# Dave Sullivan

Dave Sullivan, the third boy of eight children, was raised in beautiful Ashland, Oregon, home of the world-renowned Shakespeare Festival. Dave has enjoyed an adventurous media career. He's been a major market television anchor, executive producer of commercials and corporate films, business owner/manager, marketing consultant, and is presently heading up business development for Perkins & Company, Oregon's largest locally owned accounting/advisory firm.

Dave has earned a reputation as a dynamic leader by combining creativity, humor, and a zest for life with sound business strategy. His greatest joy is spending time with his equally energetic wife, Sally, a health educator, registered nurse, and pharmaceutical representative, and their three active children, Scott, Christopher, and Julie.

DAVE SULLIVAN'S TEACHER WITH CLASS IS
## ৡ MRS. MORRIS

# MRS. MORRIS

My first four years of grade school were spent in a private Catholic school where I was taught by nuns. When my parents announced that I would be attending a public grade school in fifth grade, I was quite concerned and nervous. Would the kids like me? Would I like the kids? Would I like my teacher? I walked in feeling like a complete basket case the first day of fifth grade.

Then I saw her. To me, Mrs. Morris looked like a universal grandma . . . silver white hair, sparkling eyes and rosy cheeks. I still remember what she was wearing on my first day—a dark blue, calf-length dress with white flowers. I felt safe.

Mrs. Morris made sure the nervous new kid from St. Mary's was embraced, nurtured, and challenged to new heights of excellence in her class at Briscoe Elementary School.

On paper I always looked like a good student or at least my report cards showed high marks. But, at my young age, I hadn't yet hit my stride in developing study habits and knowing that I had a brain. Based on my parent's assessment, I could achieve great things. I just wasn't quite sure how I was going to go about it.

Perhaps Mrs. Morris's greatest gift to me and all her students over decades of teaching was providing an environment for her students to flourish. I remember one particularly miserable day when I was still trying to fit in with my new classmates and feeling terribly homesick for my old school. Class had just ended.

Students were quickly filing out when she called my name. Was I in trouble? No, her soft warm eyes assured me everything was fine. I crept up to her desk and I remember the words she spoke to me that day, as if they were just spoken.

"People will judge you your whole life. Ignore those judgments. Your true friends will look inside, to your heart, past your looks or outside appearances. Be proud of who you are." With those words, a feeling of complete reassurance came over me. My own sense of excellence began in grade school, not graduate school.

Mrs. Morris created a classroom with direction and clear expectations. The environment in her classroom was one of high standards. Imagine that! Perfect modeling for the "real world." She knew it, we did not, but we benefited from it. From that first nervous day in fifth grade, Mrs. Morris offered and reinforced the notion that I could achieve great things . . . no subject was too difficult to master. Although I was living in a small rural town, she showed me how to open my mind to the larger world in front of me. Mrs. Morris, the grandmother in a blue dress, enabled me to see beyond my hometown of Ashland, Oregon.

As the years passed and I moved on to high school, college, a career, marriage, and three children, Mrs. Morris was with me . . . my litmus test for excellence. Over three decades have passed and now my daughter, Julie, is about to start fifth grade. I sincerely hope there is another Mrs. Morris out there for my Julie, a teacher who does more to encourage and help the next generation than any politician, CEO, or dotcom website. ❦

*One looks back with appreciation to the brilliant teachers, but with gratitude to those who touched our human feelings. The curriculum is so much necessary raw material, but warmth is the vital element for the growing plant and for the soul of the child.*

**— Carl Jung**

# Amanda Jane Peach

Amanda Jane Peach still doesn't know very much about grammar or remember many of the details about Shakespeare, Nathaniel Hawthorne, or Mark Twain. However, she enjoys reading and writing as well as smelling the roses growing along the picket fence of her home in Lake Oswego, Oregon, where she has lived with her family for the past twelve years. When not found with a pen and notebook in hand, Amanda often enjoys playing guitar, writing letters, and spending time at church—a central part of her life. In the fall of 2001, Amanda began her college studies at Azusa Pacific University in Southern California. She is thankful for role models such as Dr. Korach who have taught her that beauty is often found in unexpected places, and that the best essays aren't always the longest.

AMANDA JANE PEACH'S TEACHER WITH CLASS IS
℘ DR. KORACH

# Dr. Korach

*I* love flowers. To me even simple dandelions convey the symbol of life, a message of rebirth and energy. So, I was delighted to walk into my English class the first day of junior year and see a tiny bouquet on each of the shiny round tables around the room. It was evident that my teacher also loved flowers.

My printed schedule of classes read "Dr. Korach" next to Honors English for second period, and after looking around the room, I spotted my instructor-to-be poised attentively behind her speaking podium. Dr. Korach wasn't all that easy to find in the sea of sixteen- and seventeen-year-olds crowding the room, as she was no more than five foot three. I was curious about my new teacher, not to mention a little intimidated. I found a seat in the corner and watched her nod and smile politely as my fellow classmates continued to file into the room. I did not realize what would transpire between my first meeting with Dr. Korach in September and our final good-byes in June. Little did I know that this bushy-haired woman in thick glasses and dangling earrings would become the best teacher I ever had . . . not to mention, one of my heroes.

The word through the grapevine was that Honors English junior year was a killer class. Maybe even the hardest class in the school. I had heard rumors of having to turn in homework even on days when the class wasn't in session. Not surprisingly, the grapevine didn't lie and I soon found the assignments consuming the tiny lines of my assignment book and spilling out into the margins. I quickly learned that there was no going easy in Dr. Korach's class. If one wanted to be a good student it was either all or nothing. I decided to give her my all.

Her assignments resulted in late nights, toiling over just the right choice of words. While she may have been strict with the proper demonstration of sentence structure and grammar tools (my worst areas), Dr. Korach was open to new ideas. She was willing to work with even a slightly bizarre thesis, returning a genuine investment of her time and insight. Dr. Korach treated us as fellow colleagues, and viewed her class as a chance to learn from those she instructed. As a result of her interest in us as writers, I didn't dare turn in anything but my best. When Dr. Korach handed back my papers and the margins were packed with strings of penciled commentary, I devoured the critique. Did she think that line was good? Did she see the value of my conclusions? Paper after paper, Dr. Korach pumped newfound confidence into me. Read this! Write this! Analyze! Criticize! My late-night explorations were all about finding the real answers to Dr. Korach's questions. She never held back in her daring challenges. In fact, she asked more of me.

Sometimes when I thought I had just figured something out, Dr. Korach would challenge us to think harder and deeper. She stood behind the old podium appearing like a fire and brimstone preacher. In sudden bursts of enthusiasm, Dr. Korach would often pace excitedly in front of the class, or swiftly turn to the whiteboard to diagram a sentence, write a quote, or illustrate the harmony of yin and yang.

As I got to know her more, Dr. Korach gave me a better appreciation of life.

I came to admire her wisdom and confidence. In her form I saw a role model of substance. On the first day of English my junior year of high school, I thought I had little else in common with my teacher besides a love of flowers. On the last day of English that year, I walked out of her classroom with a deeper love and appreciation of literature than I had ever found before. In that same classroom with flowers atop the shiny, round tables, I had also found myself a hero. ❧

# Mike Rich

Mike Rich wrote the screenplay for the film *The Rookie*, a box-office hit about a teacher and coach that was released in the spring of 2002.

He also wrote the screenplay for *Finding Forrester*, a film that pays tribute to the power of mentoring and the joy that comes from putting our thoughts on paper. He is currently working on a variety of film projects from his home in Beaverton, Oregon, and was selected by *Variety* magazine as one of "Ten Screenwriters to Watch."

MIKE RICH'S TEACHER WITH CLASS IS
&#x2767; MRS. FORSTER

# Mrs. Forster

*I*'m often asked where the lessons came from in *Finding Forrester*. Who taught me to "write your first draft with your heart and rewrite with your head." Who pushed me, encouraged me, to view writing not as a chore, but to see it as a wondrous release that would last a lifetime.

And when I'm asked that question, I tell them about Sharon Forster, my high school English teacher in Enterprise, Oregon. If there was a Mr. Holland in Enterprise, a tiny rural town in the northeastern part of the state, it was Mrs. Forster. She was the type of educator who saw lecturing as only part of the process, an educator who felt that showing things to her students was just as important.

My senior class made a trip to the Shakespearean festival in Ashland, no small journey considering that Enterprise and Ashland are about as far apart as two towns in the same state can be. She taught us not to be afraid of ending a sentence with "be," or starting one with "and" or "but." Rules are precious, but every once in awhile, breaking those rules puts a new color in the portrait.

I recall one writing assignment early in my senior year. Being as we had only forty kids in the entire senior class, I found myself to be a fairly solid proponent of grading-on-the-curve. The paper I handed in reflected as much. It was mediocre at best. And Mrs. Forster didn't hesitate to label it with a C-minus, a grade that paled in comparison to the B's and B-pluses I saw floating on the desks of those around me.

I complained about the grade, challenging her to tell me that the paper wasn't the best in the entire class. She confirmed that it was but added that it simply wasn't my best.

I recall leaving for college that fall, Mrs. Forster's handprints still on my back from the times she pushed me to excel in, to enjoy, my writing. I reacted as any eighteen-year-old would; shrugging the encouragement away, worrying about the upcoming Friday night activities.

What I didn't realize is that the seeds of writing had already been planted and that they would continue to push their way to the surface every few months. A short story here, a short story there.

In early 1997, I tried my hand at screenwriting, the story of a reclusive writer and his unexpected friendship with a young man from the Bronx gnawing away in my head. In the months following the release of *Finding Forrester*, I often found myself being praised for naming the lead character after my teacher, as if I was the one who had extended the gift.

All great stories start with a teacher. All great stories end with their ongoing influence. ❧

*My heart is singing for joy this morning. A miracle has happened! The light of understanding has shone upon my little pupil's mind, and behold, all things are changed!*

**— Annie Sullivan**

# Peter Pelham

Peter Pelham is an educator and an internationalist. Educated at Williams College, where he later worked as Associate Director of Admissions and Faculty Advisor to foreign students, he went on to earn graduate degrees from Harvard and the University of Virginia. In 1962, at age thirty-one, Peter was appointed president of Mount Vernon College and Seminary in Washington, D.C., a position he held for fifteen years. Subsequently he served as vice president of the Institute of International Education (IIE) and director of its Washington office.

In 1982, Peter and his wife, Isobel, founded Pelham Associates, an educational advising group located in Maryland. Pelham Associates has advised several British universities and polytechnics on collaborative agreements with U.S. higher educational institutions, and undertaken a number of overseas assignments in Africa, the Middle East, the Balkans, and Southeast Asia for a range of U.S. government agencies and NGOs. Peter is the founding President of The Global Connections Foundation, a growing network of two hundred national schools in forty-one countries worldwide.

PETER PELHAM'S TEACHER WITH CLASS IS
❤ MALCOLM McKENZIE

# MALCOLM MCKENZIE

*I* have learned considerably from the life and teachings of Malcolm McKenzie. Although my junior by some thirty years, Malcolm has the wisdom and vision of a contemporary. The "classroom" we have shared has been that of life and the process of learning. As the product of a New England upbringing and schooling, I have gradually obtained a more global mindset, one that still employs the ethics of my heritage while enjoying the instruction of such colleagues as Malcolm. Graduate studies at Harvard and the University of Virginia have not provided the insights of lessons learned from life or from those who have undergone other kinds of transformations. It is a pleasure, therefore, to share briefly this image of a world-class teacher and one whose teachings are of and about the world.

Malcolm McKenzie is a man of principle and integrity. He also has a wicked sense of humor. He is a redheaded South African. Even without his red hair and freckles, he is funny. When he smiles, his entire face lights up. He has an amazingly boyish face for someone in his forties and for someone who was exiled from his homeland early in his teaching career. It is equally amazing that the youthful visage shows few signs of the internal memory of exile. However, it is there and reflected in his keen sense of principle and integrity.

As he is a Rhodes Scholar from South Africa, one might suppose his ability to express himself was an early gift. However, in Malcolm's case, while the judicial genes of his father undoubtedly provided their own worth, it was the life lived and learned that contributed much to his clarity of thought and speech.

For Malcolm, scholarly achievements were augmented by human endeavors. In the end, though, it was the impact of man's inhumanity to man that added a special dimension to his ability to articulate—to articulate with clarity and vision to students and teachers alike on the importance of principle and integrity, of equality and good sportsmanship, of justice and truth not only in concept, but in practice.

Malcolm's transformation paralleled that of his native country. His exile for over a decade gave that transformation extra strength even beyond being named a Rhodes Scholar, the Principal of the Maru a Pula School in Botswana, or Bicentennial Fellow to Deerfield Academy in Massachusetts. That transformation resulted in his deep commitment to integrity and principle. ❦

*Modern cynics and skeptics . . .
see no harm in paying those
to whom they entrust the minds of
their children a smaller wage than
is paid to those whom they entrust
the care of their plumbing.*

— **John Fitzgerald Kennedy**

# Thomas L. Friedman

Three-time Pulitzer Prize winner and world-renowned author and journalist, Thomas Friedman has traveled hundreds of thousands of miles reporting the end of the Cold War, U.S. domestic politics and foreign policy, and international economics. His Foreign Affairs column, which appears twice a week in the *New York Times*, is syndicated to seven hundred other newspapers worldwide.

A foremost authority on the Middle East, Friedman's book, *From Beirut to Jerusalem*, won both the National Book and the Overseas Press Club Awards in 1989 and was on the *New York Times* Best-Seller List for nearly twelve months. It has been published in ten different languages, including Japanese and Chinese, and is now used as a basic textbook on the Middle East in many high schools and universities. Friedman also wrote *The Lexus and the Olive Tree*, one of the best-selling business books in 1999, and the winner of the 2000 Overseas Press Club Award for best nonfiction book on foreign policy. His most recent book is titled *Longitudes and Attitudes: Exploring the World After September 11*.

Friedman graduated summa cum laude from Brandeis University with a degree in Mediterrranean Studies and received a masters degree in Modern Middle East Studies from Oxford. He lives in Bethesda, Maryland, with his wife, Ann, and their two daughters.

THOMAS L. FRIEDMAN'S TEACHER WITH CLASS IS
## ❧ HATTIE M. STEINBERG

# HATTIE M. STEINBERG

[*R*ecently] the *New York Times Magazine* published its annual review of people who died last year who left a particular mark on the world. I am sure all readers have their own such list. I certainly do. Indeed, someone who made the most important difference in my life died last year—my high school journalism teacher, Hattie M. Steinberg.

I grew up in a small suburb of Minneapolis, and Hattie was the legendary journalism teacher at St. Louis Park High School, Room 313. I took her Intro to Journalism course in tenth grade, back in 1969, and have never needed, or taken, another course in journalism since. She was that good.

Hattie was a woman who believed that the secret for success in life was getting the fundamentals right.

And boy, she pounded the fundamentals of journalism into her students—not simply how to write a lead or accurately transcribe a quote, but, more important, how to comport yourself in a professional way and to always do quality work. To this day, when I forget to wear a tie on assignment, I think of Hattie scolding me. I once interviewed an ad exec for our high school paper who used a four-letter word. We debated whether to run it. Hattie ruled yes. That ad man almost lost his job when it appeared. She wanted to teach us about consequences.

Hattie was the toughest teacher I ever had. After you took her journalism course in tenth grade, you tried out for the paper, the *Echo*, which she supervised.

Competition was fierce. In eleventh grade, I didn't quite come up to her writing standards, so she made me business manager, selling ads to the local pizza parlors.

That year, though, she let me write one story. It was about an Israeli general who had been a hero in the Six-Day War, who was giving a lecture at the University of Minnesota. I covered his lecture and interviewed him briefly. His name was Ariel Sharon. First story I ever got published.

Those of us on the paper, and the yearbook that she also supervised, lived in Hattie's classroom. We hung out there before and after school. Now, you have to understand, Hattie was a single woman, nearing sixty at the time, and this was the 1960s. She was the polar opposite of "cool," but we hung around her classroom like it was a malt shop and she was Wolfman Jack. None of us could have articulated it then, but it was because we enjoyed being harangued by her, disciplined by her, and taught by her. She was a woman of clarity in an age of uncertainty.

We remained friends for thirty years, and she followed, bragged about, and critiqued every twist in my career. After she died, her friends sent me a pile of my stories that she had saved over the years. Indeed, her students were her family— only closer. Judy Harrington, one of Hattie's former students, remarked about other friends who were on Hattie's newspapers and yearbooks: "We all graduated forty-one years ago; and yet nearly each day in our lives something comes up—some mental image, some admonition that makes us think of Hattie."

Judy also told the story of one of Hattie's last birthday parties, when one man said he had to leave early to take his daughter somewhere. "Sit down," said Hattie.

"You're not leaving yet. She can just be a little late."

That was my teacher! I sit up straight just thinkin' about her.

Among the fundamentals Hattie introduced me to was the *New York Times*. Every morning it was delivered to Room 313. I had never seen it before then. Real journalists, she taught us, start their day by reading the *Times* and columnists like Anthony Lewis and James Reston.

I have been thinking about Hattie a lot this year, not just because she died on July 31, but because the lessons she imparted seem so relevant now. We've just gone through this huge dot-com-Internet-globalization bubble during which a lot of smart people got carried away and forgot the fundamentals of how you build a profitable company, a lasting portfolio, a nation state, or a thriving student. It turns out that the real secret of success in the information age is what it always was: fundamentals—reading, writing and arithmetic, church, synagogue and mosque, the rule of law and good governance.

The Internet can make you smarter, but it can't make you smart. It can extend your reach, but it will never tell you what to say at a P.T.A. meeting. These fundamentals cannot be downloaded. You can only upload them, the old-fashioned way, one by one, in places like Room 313 at St. Louis Park High. I only regret that I didn't write this when the woman who taught me all that was still alive. ❧

# Mary Anne Radmacher

Mary Anne Radmacher spends her best days crafting words and the silences in between them. She is the creative force in a company located in Salem, Oregon, called Word Garden.

Word Garden handcrafts posters, greeting cards, and a host of other things that feature the words, lettering, and designs of Mary Anne. She asserts that her associates at the Word Garden are now her best teachers and she is a student among them.

MARY ANNE RADMACHER'S TEACHER WITH CLASS IS
## ❧ MELBA DAY SPARKS

# MELBA DAY SPARKS

*M*elba Day Sparks, with her stark black hair pulled into a high French twist and her towering, intimidating posture, didn't just walk into a room, she entered it. Did she learn this on Broadway? In Europe? Was she born with this presence? I never knew. She never told. She would not answer personal questions. To any personal inquiry she would respond:

"But dear, this isn't about me, it's about you. What does that question teach you about yourself and how could you ask it with the same words but imply a different meaning?"

And then I would have a lesson in inflection and have a sense of even greater mystery about Mrs. Sparks. To the day she died her second husband did not know her age. Many of her students suspected she was ageless.

She taught me many things in the guise of performance—listening skills, sharpened intuition, timing, and humor. She made what was good in me better. In a manner that seemed effortless, she drew out qualities and abilities of which I was unaware. She consistently attributed the credit for all these discoveries to me.

I am uncertain how Mrs. Sparks knew my home life was challenged, and that I had lost my mother to a heart attack. As I reflect, I am uncertain how she knew the dozens of things about me that she did.

I had a habit of apologizing for most everything. In fact, I apologized for things I didn't do. I apologized for things that other people did. During our first quarter she simply and quietly said, "You must stop this." The second quarter she moved to, "You WILL stop this." And she shook her finger at me, which seemed to pierce the center of my brain.

I cannot remember why I apologized in the dressing room where we were learning the art of repairing stage makeup in the near dark. Apparently from out of nowhere her elegant fingers clasped my jaw. Through what sounded like clenched teeth, she hissed;

*"If you have wronged someone, make amends. If you have broken something, fix it. If you have caused harm, seek forgiveness. But you, Mary Anne, you must stop apologizing. For at the heart of it, you are apologizing for yourself. And for that, you have no reason. You, YOU," my head shook as she emphasized her point, "are a jewel, a shining jewel. I see it. You must see it for yourself. STOP. If you apologize again, within my hearing, I will not allow you to return to the theater department. Do you understand me?"*

She moved my head up and down. In a dark spin, she disappeared. At the time, I only understood the consequence of her comment, not her intent. I did, immediately, stop apologizing. Theater meant too much to me to not still my tongue from the familiar, "I'm sorry."

Later on, I began to grasp that Melba Day Sparks's heart saw into my home and saw me, the youngest of a much older household of siblings, always having to apologize for being "in the way." The absence of my constant apologizing created room in my life for confidence and a nascent strength. Many times, at the start of an apology, I would hear the hiss of Melba's voice, "Stop!" What impact her voice had . . . over decades. Melba Day Sparks—the teacher who walked into my life and, by her remarkable insight and presence commanded my respect, admiration, and lifelong gratitude for all the ways she taught me to proudly reach into myself, and teach myself. ∾

# *John Callahan*

John Callahan is a renowned syndicated cartoonist whose work has appeared in over fifty publications, including the *New York Daily News, Harper's*, the *Miami Herald, Seattle Times, San Diego Union*, and *San Francisco Chronicle*. Profiled on *60 Minutes* and featured in a *New York Times Magazine* cover story, his cartoons tend to reflect his unique perspective on life. Although sometimes appearing somewhat bizarre, his humor has been shaped in part by a car accident that left him a quadriplegic in 1972. Callahan, who lives in Portland, Oregon, has published several cartoon collections, including *Do Not Disturb Any Further, Digesting the Child Within*, and *Do What He Says! He's Crazy!!!*, and *Freaks of Nature*. He has also authored a children's book and the autobiography *Don't Worry, He Won't Get Far on Foot*. Matt Groening, creator of *The Simpsons*, has said of Callahan that he is "Rude, shocking depraved, tasteless—Callahan gets called all the adjectives that cartoonists crave to hear."

There are countless ways to express appreciation for a teacher and it is fitting that Mr. Callahan chose to illustrate his.

JOHN CALLAHAN'S TEACHER WITH CLASS IS
❦ **SISTER JO**

*Before* every show, I close my eyes
and say "Let's do some good here."
That's the basic lesson my father,
Bob Curry, a junior high physical
education and health teacher, taught me
way back. If I were to die tomorrow,
I know in my heart that it
mattered I was here. And that
was his greatest gift.

**— Ann Curry of NBC's Today Show**

# *Grants and Awards*
## Available for
## Our Amazing Teachers

# Raise your hand and nominate your
## *Teacher with Class!*

There are numerous grants and awards available for teachers of all levels. However, many of these are not well publicized, so while we may have good intentions to nominate a teacher with class we just don't know how to get started. Following is a partial list for your reference.

There are several options available for those interested in grants and awards:

- A colleague or student can nominate a teacher.

- Teachers can apply themselves for grants and awards that are available.

- Some grants and awards can be applied for as a group; the entire math department, for example.

The websites listed after each award will often provide links to other related websites with even more grant and award possibilities for teachers. Because awards are continuously updated, the most current information can be found on the websites. Those who prefer the telephone or good old-fashioned "snail mail" can refer to phone numbers and mailing addresses listed as well.

So . . . no more excuses, it's time to do our homework!

# THE NEA FOUNDATION FOR THE IMPROVEMENT OF EDUCATION (NFIE)

## Mission

Created by the members of the National Education Association (NEA), the NEA Foundation is a 501(c)3 public charity that empowers public education employees to innovate, take risks, and become agents for change to improve teaching and learning in our society.

## Eligibility/Award/Application Process

Guidelines and information about the NEA Foundation's grants and awards, full text of NFIE publications, and links to other resources are available at www.nfie.org or by calling 202-822-7840.

## Award

■ The NEA Foundation Learning and Leadership Grants

Purpose: To promote high-quality professional development experiences or organize a collegial study group that leads to improvements in practice, curriculum, and student achievement in U.S. public schools or higher education institutions.

■ The NEA Foundation Innovation Grants

Purpose: To promote collaborative efforts by two or more colleagues to develop and implement creative and unique ideas that result in high student achievement.

■ The NEA Foundation Award for Teaching Excellence

Purpose: To recognize, reward, and promote excellence in teaching and advocacy for the profession, and to honor public education and the dedicated members of the NEA. Nominees must be current members of their local NEA affiliate or bargaining unit. NEA state affiliates, the Federal Education Association, and direct NEA affiliates may each submit one nomination. Contact information is available from these affiliates.

## Contact Information

The NEA Foundation for the Improvement of Education
1201 Sixteenth Street, NW
Washington, DC 20036-3207
Phone:     202-822-7840
Fax:       202-822-7779
Website:   http://www.nfie.org

# All-USA Teacher Team

## Mission

*USA Today* seeks to honor teachers in all grade levels who excel in a variety of teaching situations.

## Eligibility

Teachers from urban, rural, and suburban schools, public and private, teachers of special education and gifted students, and teachers who travel to more than one school throughout the year all have been named to the First Team. Instructional teams of no more than five members can be nominated as a single entity. A teacher or instructional team may be nominated by anyone, including students, former students, parents, colleagues, staff members, or administrators.

Teachers may not be nominated without their knowledge. Self-nominations are not accepted.

## Award

$500, $2,500 for their schools, and press in *USA Today*.

## Application Process

To nominate a teacher or team, complete the nominator's statement, sign it, and give it to the nominee. The nominee(s) must complete the rest of the form.

Each nomination form must include one, and only one, nominator's statement. Either the nominator or nominee must secure two letters of recommendation in addition to the nominator's statement. To receive a nomination form, check the website or call.

## Contact Information

*USA Today*
7950 Jones Branch Drive
McLean, VA 22108-9995
Phone:     703-854-5890
           or
           800-872-0001
Website:   http://allstars.usatoday.com

# DISNEY AMERICAN TEACHER AWARDS

## Mission

Disney's American Teacher Awards is part of Disney Learning Partnership's commitment to teacher support and professional development. Disney Learning Partnership, a philanthropic initiative, supports engaging and innovative approaches to learning in classrooms across the country and draws on the resources of The Walt Disney Company. Disney feels that there is no more thoughtful gift to give a teacher who has touched a life than to recognize the role he or she has played in shaping the way a child sees the world.

## Eligibility

Disney reaches out to everyone who has been touched by the work of a creative teacher—students, parents, fellow school personnel, and members of the community are all encouraged to nominate a teacher.

## Award

- Monetary awards totaling over $500,000.
- National recognition at an Awards Gala.
- Honorees recognized at a ceremony to air on Lifetime Television.

## Application Process

Nominations can be made by phone toll free at 877-ATA-TEACH (877-282-8322) or submitted online at www.disneylearning.org.

All nominees will be contacted by Disney and will receive a copy of the American Teacher Awards application. The teacher must complete the application, which will then be reviewed by a national selection committee.

## Contact Information

Disney Hand
500 South Buena Vista Street
Burbank, CA 91521-0893
Phone:      877-ATA-TEACH (877-282-8322)
Website:    http://www.disneylearning.org

# *Education Week* on the Web and *Teacher Magazine*

## Mission

*Education Week* (on the web) and *Teacher Magazine* (in print) raise the level of awareness and understanding among professional educators and the general public, and contribute significantly to the welfare of American education. They publish a current and extensive list of grants and awards both on their website and in the magazine.

## Eligibility/Award/Application Process

Please contact the organization directly.

## Contact Information

Editorial Projects in Education, Inc.
Suite 100
6935 Arlington Road
Bethesda, MD 20814-5233
Phone:        800-346-1834
              301-280-3100
Fax for *Teacher Magazine*:    301-280-3150
Fax for *Education Week*:      301-280-3200
Fax for Business Info:         301-280-3250
Website:      http://www.edweek.org/

# ELEANOR ROOSEVELT
# TEACHER FELLOWSHIPS

## Mission

Eleanor Roosevelt Teacher Fellowships are designed to provide professional development opportunities for female public school teachers; improve girls' learning opportunities, especially in math, science, and technology; and promote equity and long-term change in classrooms, schools, and school systems.

## Eligibility

Applicants must:

- Be a U.S. citizen or permanent resident.
- Teach grades K–12 full-time in U.S. public schools.
- Have taught full-time for at least three consecutive years.
- Plan to continue teaching after the fellowship year.
- Have a commitment to furthering educational equity through classroom, school district, or community work.

## Award

Professional Development Fellowships up to $5,000 each to fund K–12 female public school teachers for professional development workshops or conferences.

- Provide seed money for these teachers to plan a gender-equity school-based program.

- Cover their attendance at the dynamic five-day Eleanor Roosevelt Teacher Institute held in Washington, D.C.

- Additional support is available for a colleague to attend the Teacher Institute.

- Project Implementation Grants up to $10,000 are available to support a classroom or school program to advance gender equity.

## Application Process

Please contact the organization directly.

## Contact Information

National Office
American Association of University Women
AAUW Educational Foundation
AAUW Legal Advocacy Fund
1111 Sixteenth Street N.W.
Washington, DC  20036
Phone:       800-326-AAUW
Fax:         202-872-1425
TDD:         202-785-7777
E-mail:      info@aauw.org
Website:     http://www.aauw.org/3000/fdnfelgra/ertf.html

# THE INTERNATIONAL READING ASSOCIATION

## Mission

The International Reading Association presents a number of awards and grants each year to recognize outstanding teachers of reading and literacy at all levels and to support teachers' efforts to enhance their knowledge and teaching skills and to make meaningful contributions to their profession.

## Eligibility/Awards/Application Process

Please contact the organization directly.

## Contact Information

International Reading Association Headquarters Office
800 Barksdale Road
Post Office Box 8139
Newark, DE 19714-8139
Phone:       302-731-1600
Fax:         302-731-1057
Website:     http://www.reading.org/about/hq.html

# Internet Innovator Award

The National Semiconductor's Internet Innovator Awards program rewards teachers who are using the Internet in fresh new ways in the classroom to improve student learning. National Semiconductor provides system-on-a-chip solutions for the information age. Combining real-world analog and state-of-the-art digital technology, the company's chips lead many sectors of the personal computer, communications, and consumer markets. Additional company and product information is available on the World Wide Web at www.national.com.

## Mission

National Semiconductor has made a commitment to training teachers to effectively use Internet technology as a resource through the Internet Training Initiative. This Initiative consists of two training programs, Global Connections and Global Connections Online, and the Internet Innovator Awards. The Awards program is expanded to recognize and reward K–12 educators across the United States who exemplify the highest level of innovation integrating Internet technology into their curriculum.

## Eligibility

Teachers who have implemented Internet-rich curricula that have proven successful in the K–12 classroom.

## Award

- Each National Semiconductor Internet Innovator, or group of Innovators, receives a check totaling $10,000 to be used at his or her discretion—no strings attached. (Groups of Innovators will divide the $10,000 award among their members.)

- $15,000 to further the use and integration of Internet technology in education.

- Airfare and accommodations to the NSBA Technology + Learning Conference in Atlanta for a special awards ceremony.

## Application Process

Two separate but similar programs offer awards on an annual basis. The difference is based on where a teacher's school is located. One is called the US-Wide Awards, and the other is the Regional Awards Program. Further details and application forms can be found at each website.

## Contact Information

E-mail to Internet Innovator Awards:  nsawards@pccinc.org
US-Wide Awards website:  http://www.nsawards.com
Regional Awards Program website:  http://www.nsawards.com/regional/index.html

# NATIONAL ENDOWMENT FOR THE HUMANITIES

## Mission

The National Endowment for the Humanities is an independent federal agency created in 1965. It is the largest founder of humanities programs in the United States. The Endowment's mission is to enrich American cultural life by promoting knowledge of human history, thought, and culture throughout the nation.

## Eligibility

NEH grants typically go to cultural institutions such as museums, archives, libraries, colleges, universities, public television and radio stations, and to individual scholars for development of high-quality humanities projects in four funding areas: preserving and providing access to cultural resources, education, research, and public programs.

## Award

Awards vary for each grant. Grants are available to:

- Preserve and provide access to cultural and educational resources essential to the American people.
- Strengthen teaching and learning in the humanities in schools and colleges across the nation.
- Facilitate research and original scholarship in the humanities.

- Provide opportunities for lifelong learning in the humanities for all Americans.

- Strengthen the institutional base of the humanities.

## Application Process

The process is somewhat different for each type of grant, so please contact the organization directly.

## Contact Information

National Endowment for the Humanities
1100 Pennsylvania Avenue, N.W.
Room 318
Washington, DC 20506
Phone:      202-606-8200
E-mail:      fellowships@neh.gov
Website:    http://www.neh.gov

# NATIONAL TEACHERS HALL OF FAME

## Mission

The mission of The National Teachers Hall of Fame is to recognize and honor exceptional teachers and the teaching profession; to promote excellence in teaching by creating a national center for the study of American education, providing opportunities to address the critical issues of our time through research and study; developing programs that will influence the recruitment and retention of quality teachers for every classroom in America; and to preserve the richness of American education as well as demonstrate exciting ventures into the future.

## Eligibility

Candidates must be certified public or nonpublic classroom teachers (active or retired) with at least twenty years' experience teaching in grades preK–12. The Hall of Fame annually honors five teachers who have demonstrated commitment and dedication to teaching our nation's children.

## Award

Inductees receive:

- A plaque bearing their picture, name, and brief description for display in their school and the Hall of Fame.
- Marlow woodcut of a country school scene.

- Signet ring and lapel pin presented by Herff Jones, Inc.

- A $1,000 stipend and a $1,000 scholarship for a student in the inductee's school district who is planning to pursue a degree in education presented by Horace Mann.

- $1,000 in materials for their school district from Scott Foresman/ Prentice Hall.

- $1,000 in gift certificates for their school from Successories.

- A permanent display in The National Teachers Hall of Fame.

- A cast bronze belltower award.

## Application Process

Anyone may nominate a teacher by obtaining and submitting a completed nomination form. The form can now be accessed online. Nomination forms may be obtained by calling or by writing The National Teachers Hall of Fame.

## Contact Information

The National Teachers Hall of Fame
1320 C of E Drive
Emporia, KS 66801
Phone:        800-96-TEACH or 620-341-9131
Website:      http://www.nthf.org/teacher.htm

# THE STATE AND NATIONAL
# TEACHER OF THE YEAR PROGRAM

The State and National Teacher of the Year Program is sponsored by the Council of Chief State School Officers (CCSSO) and Scholastic Inc., the global children's publishing and media company. The program focuses public attention on teaching excellence and is the oldest and most prestigious awards program for teachers.

## Eligibility

Teachers from each of the fifty states, five U.S. extra-state jurisdictions, the District of Columbia, and the Department of Defense Dependents Schools.

## Award

The National Teacher of the Year is released from classroom duties during the year of recognition to travel nationally and internationally as a spokesperson for the teaching profession. All activities of the National Teacher, and projects involving the State Teachers of the Year, are coordinated through the National Teacher of the Year Program.

## Application process

### National Level:

Each state candidate submits:

- Written application containing biographical and professional information.

- Eight essays on topics ranging from personal teaching philosophy to the issues facing education.
- Letters of endorsement.

**Early December:** National Selection Committee meets to choose four finalists from nominations received.

**Late February:** Personal interviews with the finalists in Washington, D.C.

**April:** National Teacher selected and introduced to the nation by the President and honored in a series of events in Washington, D.C.

## State Level:

Each year, fifty states, five U.S. extra-state jurisdictions, the District of Columbia, and the Department of Defense Dependents Schools name a state teacher of the year.

- Selection processes varies within the states
- You may select State Teacher of the Year Program Coordinators to access information about your state's coordinator. The list is organized alphabetically by state. Participation in the National Teacher of the Year Program is available through your State Teacher of the Year Program.

## Contact Information

National Teacher of the Year Program Office
Council of Chief State School Officers
One Massachusetts Avenue, NW, Suite 700
Washington, D.C. 20001-1431
Phone:     202-336-7047
Fax:       202-408-8081
Website:   http://www.ccsso.org/ntoy.html

# State Teacher of the Year Program Coordinators

Upon publication date the following information is current. If your State Teacher of the Year Coordinator has been changed, please contact the National Teacher of the Year Program Office and request the name and number of your current state coordinator, or go to their website, which has links to all State Teacher of the Year Coordinators.

## Alabama

Ann Starks
Teacher of the Year Coordinator
State Department of Education
5303 Gordon Persons Building
50 North Ripley Street
Montgomery, AL 36130
Phone:    334-242-9702
Fax:        334-353-4682
E-mail:   astarks@alsde.edu

## Alaska

Helen Mehrkens
Teacher of the Year Coordinator
Educational Administrator,
   Program Division
Alaska Department of Education
801 West 10th Street
Juneau, AK 99801-1894
Phone:   907-465-8730
Fax:        907-465-3396
E-mail:   helen_mehrkens@educ.state.ak.us

## American Samoa

Filemoni Lauilefue
Teacher of the Year Coordinator
Department of Education
Post Office Box 1132
Pago Pago, AS 96799
Phone:   011-684-699-1836
Fax:        011-684-633-5752
E-mail:   filemonil@doe.as

## Arizona

Bobbie O'Boyle
Teacher of the Year Coordinator
Executive Director
Arizona Educational Foundation
6320 East Thomas Road, Suite 307
Scottsdale, AZ 85251
Phone:   480-421-9376
Fax:        480-421-9809
E-mail:   bobbie@azedfoundation.org

## Arkansas

Charles D. Watson
Teacher of the Year Coordinator
State Department of Education
Systems Planning & Support
Four State Capitol Mall
Little Rock, AR 72201-1071
Phone: 501-682-4474
Fax: 501-682-5162
E-mail: cwatson@arkedu.k12.ar.us

## California

Kim Edwards
Consultant
State Department of Education
721 Capitol Mall
Sacramento, CA 95814
Phone: 916-657-4845
Fax: 916-657-5301
E-mail: kedwards@cde.ca.gov

## Colorado

Jody Ohmert Nordbye
Teacher of the Year Coordinator
State Department of Education
201 East Colfax Avenue
Denver, CO 80203-1799
Phone: 303-866-6937
Fax: 303-866-6938
E-mail: nordbye_j@cde.state.co.us

## Connecticut

Gregory Kane
Supervisor of Technical Education
Teacher of the Year Coordinator
State Department of Education
Post Office Box 2219
Hartford, CT 06145-2219
Phone: 860-713-6756
Fax: 860-713-7018
E-mail: gregory.kane@po.state.ct.us

## Delaware

Betty Torbert
Teacher of the Year Coordinator
State Department of Public Instruction
Townsend Building
Post Office Box 1402
Dover, DE 19903
Phone: 302-739-4602
Fax: 302-739-4654
E-mail: btorbert@state.de.us

## Department of Defense Education Activity (DoDEA)

Carol Drechsel
Professional Development Specialist
Teacher of the Year Coordinator
Professional Development Division
Department of Defense Education Activity
4040 North Fairfax Drive, Room 4-60
Arlington, VA 22203
Phone: 703-696-4414, ext. 4133
Fax: 703-696-8956
E-mail: cdrechse@hq.dodea.edu

## District of Columbia

Carolyn Pinckney
Teacher of the Year Coordinator
Coordinator of Teacher Affairs
District of Columbia Public Schools
825 North Capitol Avenue, Suite 9051
Washington, DC 20002
Phone: 202-442-5616
Fax: 202-442-5017
E-mail: carolyn.pinckney@k12.dc.us

## Florida

Olga Gary
Teacher of the Year Coordinator
State Department of Education
325 West Gaines Street, Suite 124
Tallahassee, FL 32399-0400
Phone: 850-922-9750
Fax: 850-413-0026
E-mail: garyo@mail.doe.state.fl.us

## Georgia

Judy Floyd
Teacher of the Year Coordinator
State Department of Education
205 Butler Street, SE
2054 Twin Towers East
Atlanta, GA 30334-5010
Phone: 404-657-2949
Fax: 404-657-6867
E-mail: judyfloyd@doe.k12.ga.us

## Guam

Tony Diaz
Teacher of the Year Coordinator
Department of Education
Post Office Box DE
Agana, GU 96932
Phone: 011-671-475-0458
Fax: 011-671-472-5003
E-mail: tdiaz@doe.edu.gu

## Hawaii

Elizabeth Wong
Teacher of the Year Coordinator
Affirmative Action Coordinator
State Department of Education
Post Office Box 2360
Honolulu, HI 96804
Phone: 808-586-3280
Fax: 808-586-3419
E-mail: Elizabeth_Wong@notes.k12.hi.us

## Idaho

Allison Westfall
Teacher of the Year Coordinator
Public Information Officer
State Department of Education
Office of the Superintendent
Post Office Box 83702
650 West State Street
Boise, ID 83720-0027
Phone: 208-332-6800
Fax: 208-334-2228
E-mail: awestfal@sde.state.id.us

## Illinois

Kim Knauer and Ann Keran
Teacher of the Year Coordinators
State Board of Education
100 North First Street
Springfield, IL 62777-0001
Phone: 217-782-4648
Fax: 217-524-8585
E-mail: kknauer@isbe.net
        akeran@isbe.net

## Indiana

Cathy Danyluk
Teacher of the Year Coordinator
State Department of Education
Room 229, State House
Indianapolis, IN 46214-2798
Phone: 317-232-9150
Fax: 317-232-9140
E-mail: cdanyluk@doe.state.in.us

## Iowa

David Winans
Teacher of the Year Coordinator
State Department of Education
Grimes State Office Building
Des Moines, IA 50319-0146
Phone: 515-281-3605
Fax: 515-281-7669
E-mail: david.winans@ed.state.ia.us

## Kansas

Sherry Bukovatz
Teacher of the Year Coordinator
State Department of Education
120 Southeast Tenth Avenue
Topeka, KS 66612-1182
Phone: 785-296-4876
Fax: 785-296-7933
E-mail: sbukovatz@ksbe.org

## Kentucky

Donna Melton
Teacher of the Year Coordinator
Program Consultant
State Department of Education
500 Mero Street, 19th Floor
Frankfort, KY 40601
Phone: 502-564-3421
Fax: 502-564-6470
E-mail: dmelton@kde.state.ky.us

## Louisiana

Gladys Kopp
Education Program Specialist
Teacher of the Year Coordinator
State Department of Education
Post Office Box 94064
626 North 4th Street
Baton Rouge, LA 70804-9064
Phone: 225-342-3383
Fax: 225-342-7367
E-mail: gkopp@mail.doe.state.la.us

## Maine

David Cadigan
Teacher of the Year Coordinator
State Department of Education
#23 State House Station
Augusta, ME 04333-0023
Phone: 207-624-6636
Fax: 207-624-6841
E-mail: david.cadigan@state.me.us

## Maryland

Darla Strouse
Teacher of the Year Coordinator
Director
Partnerships, Research & Development
State Department of Education
200 West Baltimore Street, 5th Floor
Baltimore, MD 21201
Phone: 410-767-0369
Fax: 410-333-3867
E-mail: dstrouse@msde.state.md.us

## Massachusetts

Deborah Walker
Teacher of the Year Coordinator
State Department of Education
350 Main Street, Fifth Floor
Malden, MA 02148
Phone: 781-338-3347
Fax: 781-338-3396
E-mail: djwalker@doe.mass.edu

## Michigan

Cheryl Poole
Consultant, Professional Development
Teacher of the Year Coordinator
State Department of Education
Box 30008
Lansing, MI 48933
Phone: 517-241-4546
Fax: 517-335-0592
E-mail: poolecl@state.mi.us

## Minnesota

Tom Nordby
Teacher of the Year Coordinator
Communications Specialist
Education Minnesota
41 Sherburne Avenue
St. Paul, MN 55103-6969
Phone: 651-292-4816, 800-652-9073
Fax: 651-292-4868
E-mail: tnordby@educationminnesota.org

## Mississippi

Daphne Buckley and Cecily McNair
Teacher of the Year Co-Coordinators
Mississippi Teacher Center
State Department of Education
359 Northwest Street, Suite 145
Jackson, MS 39201
Phone: 601-359-3631
Fax: 601-359-1728
E-mail: dbuckley@mde.k12.ms.us
cmcnair@mde.k12.ms.us

## Missouri

Jean Cole
Teacher of the Year Coordinator
Department of Elementary &
  Secondary Education
Post Office Box 480
Jefferson State Office Building
Jefferson City, MO  65102-0480
Phone:  573-751-2661
Fax:    573-526-4261
E-mail:  jcole@mail.dese.state.mo.us

## Montana

Judy McMaster
Teacher of the Year Coordinator
Montana Education Association
1232 East Sixth Avenue
Helena, MT  59601
Phone:  406-442-4250
Fax:    406-443-5081
E-mail:  jmcmaster@mea-mft.org

## Nebraska

Beverly Newton, Dave Ankenman, and
  Ann Masters
Teacher of the Year Coordinators
State Department of Education
Post Office Box 94987
301 Centennial Mall South
Lincoln, NE  68509-4987
Phone:  402-471-4865
Fax:    402-471-0117
E-mail:  bnewton@nde.state.ne.us
         ankenman@nde.state.ne.us

## Nevada

Mary Geisler
Teacher of the Year Program Coordinator
State Department of Education
700 East 5th Street
Carson City, NV  89701-5050
Phone:  775-687-9224
Fax:    775-687-9202
E-mail:  mgeisler@nsn.k12.nv.us

## New Hampshire

Lori Perriello
Teacher of the Year Coordinator
State Department of Education
101 Pleasant Street
State Office Park South
Concord, NH  03301
Phone:  603-271-8315
Fax:    603-271-1953
E-mail:  lperriello@ed.state.nh.us

## New Jersey

Susan Sliker
Teacher of the Year Coordinator
Education Program Specialist
State Department of Education
100 Riverview Plaza, CN 500
Trenton, NJ 08625-0500
Phone:  609-984-6314
Fax:    609-292-3142
E-mail:  sue.sliker@doe.state.nj.us

### New Mexico

Vicki Breen
Teacher of the Year Coordinator
State Department of Education
Education Building
300 Don Gaspar
Santa Fe, NM  87501-2786
Phone:   505-827-6559
Fax:       505-827-6694
E-mail:  vbreen@sde.state.nm.us

Pat Graff
President, NM State Teachers of the Year
Teacher of the Year Coordinator
La Cueva High School
8101 Krim, NE
Albuquerque, NM 87109
Phone:   505-821-2331
Fax:       404-797-2250
E-mail:  pgraff@aol.com

### New York

Cheryl Fries
Teacher of the Year Coordinator
Assistant in Higher Education
State Department of Education
Professional Career Opportunity
   Programs Bureau
Room 962 EBA
Albany, NY 12234
Phone:   518-486-6042
Fax:       518-486-3239
E-mail:  cfries@mail.nysed.gov

### North Carolina

Cecil Banks
Teacher of the Year Coordinator
Coordinator, Recruitment Activities
Center for Recruitment and Retention
State Department of Public Instruction
Education Building
301 North Wilmington Street
Raleigh, NC  27601-2825
Phone:   919-807-3375
Fax:       919-807-3362
E-mail:  cbanks@dpi.state.nc.us

### North Dakota

LeAnn Nelson
Teacher of the Year Coordinator
Director of Professional Development
North Dakota Education Association
Post Office Box 5005
Bismarck, ND 58501
Phone:   701-223-0450 ext. 102
Fax:       701-224-8535
E-mail:  leann.nelson@ndea.org

### Northern Mariana Islands

Lou Mendiola
Teacher of the Year Coordinator
Department of Education
Post Office Box 1370
Chalan Kanoa
Saipan, MP  96950
Phone:   670-664-3770
Fax:       670-664-3798
E-mail:  loumendiola@hotmail.com

## Ohio

Kim Kehl
Teacher of the Year Coordinator
Administrator
Ohio Department of Education
Center for the Teaching Profession
25 South Front Street, Mail Stop 505
Columbus, OH 43215-4183
Phone:   614-466-5795
Fax:       614-728-3058
E-mail:   kim.kehl@ode.state.oh.us

## Oklahoma

Linda Ruhman
Teacher of the Year Coordinator
Director, Residency/
    Professional Development
State Department of Education
Hodge Education Building
2500 North Lincoln Boulevard, Suite 212
Oklahoma City, OK  73105-4599
Phone:   405-521-4527
Fax:       405-521-6205
E-mail:   Linda_Ruhman@mail.sde.state.ok.us
               patti_meier@mail.sde.state.ok.us

## Oregon

Rob Larson
Teacher of the Year Coordinator
Policy & Research analyst
State Department of Education
Public Service Building
255 Capitol Street, NE
Salem, OR  97310-0203
Phone:   503-378-3600, ext. 2354
Fax:       503-378-5156
E-mail:   rob.larson@state.or.us

Nanci Schneider
Teacher of the Year Coordinator
Director, School and District Report Card
State Department of Education
Public Service Building
255 Capitol Street, NE
Salem, OR  97310-0203
Phone:   503-378-3600, ext. 2353
Fax:       503-378-5156
E-mail:   nanci.schneider@state.or.us

## Pennsylvania

Dr. Parker Martin
Teacher of the Year Coordinator
Division of School Improvement
Pennsylvania Department of Education
333 Market Street, 8th Floor
Harrisburg, PA  17126-0333
Phone:   717-783-4307
Fax:       717-783-6617
E-mail:   pamartin@state.pa.us

## Puerto Rico

Pablo Rivera
Teacher of the Year Coordinator
Puerto Rico Department of Education
Post Office Box 190759
San Juan, PR 00919-0759
Phone: 787-759-2000, ext. 2687
Fax: 787-753-1804

## Rhode Island

Doris Anselmo
Teacher of the Year Coordinator
Interim Director
Office of Teacher Preparation, Certification
   and Professional Development
Rhode Island Department of Education
255 Westminster Street, Shepard Building
Providence, RI 02903-3400
Phone: 401-277-4600, ext. 2252
Fax: 401-277-2048
E-mail: ride1503@ride.ri.net

## South Carolina

Barbara Ann Walker
Teacher of the Year Coordinator
Division of Teacher Quality
State Department of Education
1600 Gervais Street
Columbia, SC 29201
Phone: 803-734-3392
Fax: 803-734-3389
E-mail: bawalker@scteachers.org

## South Dakota

Terri Cordrey
Teacher of the Year Coordinator
Office of Technical Assistance
700 Governors Drive
Kneip Building
Pierre, SD 57501-2291
Phone: 605-773-4662
Fax: 605-773-3782
E-mail: terri.cordrey@state.sd.us

## Tennessee

Cindy Fagan Benefield
Teacher of the Year Coordinator
Tennessee Department of Education
710 James Robertson Parkway
Nashville, TN 37243
Phone: 615-532-4712
Fax: 615-532-8312
E-mail: cindy.benefield@state.tn.us

## Texas

Marilyn Kuelhem
Teacher of the Year Coordinator
Texas Education Agency
William B. Travis Building
1701 North Congress Avenue, Room 2-180
Austin, TX 78701-1494
Phone: 512-463-9000
Fax: 512-463-5947
E-mail: mkuelhem@tea.state.tx.us

## Utah

Mark Peterson
Teacher of the Year Coordinator
Utah State Office of Education
2500 East 500 South
Post Office Box 144200
Salt Lake City, UT 84414-4200
Phone:   801-538-7525
Fax:       801-538-7768
E-mail:   mpeterso@usoe.k12.ut.us

## Vermont

Deb Armitage
Teacher of the Year Coordinator
Department of Professional Development
State Department of Education
120 State Street, 5th Floor
Montpelier, VT 05620-2501
Phone:   802-828-5409
Fax:       802-828-3146
E-mail:   darmitage@doe.state.vt.us

## Virginia

Bryd Latham
Teacher of the Year Coordinator
State Department of Education
Post Office Box 2120
Richmond, VA  23218-2120
Phone:   804-225-2104
Fax:       804-786-6759
E-mail:   blatham@pen.k12.va.us

## Virgin Islands

William Frett
Teacher of the Year Coordinator
Insular Superintendent
St. Thomas/St. Johns District Schools
44-46 Kongens Gade
St. Thomas, VI  00802
Phone:   340-776-2250, ext. 244
Fax:       340-775-7381
E-mail:   wfrett@sttj.k12.vi.us

## Washington

Julie Hanson
Teacher of the Year Coordinator
State Department of Public Instruction
Old Capitol Building
Post Office Box 47200
Olympia, WA  98516
Phone:   360-586-3186
Fax:       360-586-0247
E-mail:   jhanson@ospi.wednet.edu

## West Virginia

Tony Smedley
Teacher of the Year Coordinator
State Department of Education
Office of Professional Development
1900 Kanawha Boulevard, East
Building 6, Room 262
Charleston, WV  25305-0330
Phone:   304-558-2702
Fax:       304-558-0882
E-mail:   tsmedley@access.k12.wv.us

## Wisconsin

Greg Doyle
Teacher of the Year Coordinator
Director, Public Information Services
State Department of Public Instruction
125 South Webster Street
Post Office Box 7841
Madison, WI  53707-7841
Phone:   608-266-1098
Fax:        608-264-9328
E-mail:   greg.doyle@dpi.state.wi.us

## Wyoming

Faith Camargo
Teacher of the Year Coordinator
State Department of Education
Hathaway Building, Second Floor
2300 Capitol Avenue
Cheyenne, WY  82002-0050
Phone:   307-777-7675
Fax:        307-777-6234
E-mail:   fcamar@educ.state.wy.us

# TARGET TEACHER SCHOLARSHIPS

## Mission

Every year, Target gives millions of dollars to deserving students, teachers, and schools across the country to help support and enhance their education efforts.

Since 1998, Target has supported teachers with over $4 million in scholarships for enhancing their education.

## Eligibility/Awards/Application Process

The details of these scholarships change each year. For more information, call or stop by your local Target Store and pick up a brochure.

## Contact Information

Phone:    800-316-6142
Website:  http://www.target.com

# TEACHING TOLERANCE GRANT PROGRAM

Teaching Tolerance grants are made possible by gifts from supporters of Southern Poverty Law Center.

## Eligibility

The Teaching Tolerance project of the Southern Poverty Law Center offers grants to K–12 classroom teachers for implementing tolerance projects in their schools and communities.

## Award

Grants up to $2,000.

## Application Process

No deadline for proposals.

Application Proposals must use the Teaching Tolerance Grant Application Form (can be downloaded from website) and should contain the following:

- A contact person (one person only).
- A detailed budget.
- A one-to-two page (maximum) narrative.

If proposal is accepted, teacher must submit a follow-up report telling how the project was implemented and the effect it had on school and community.

## Contact Information

Grants Administrator
Teaching Tolerance Grants
c/o The Southern Poverty Law Center
400 Washington Avenue
Montgomery, AL 36104
Phone:      334-956-8200
Fax:        334-956-8488
Website:    http://www.tolerance.org

# The National Science Teacher Association (NSTA)

## Mission

The National Science Teachers Association (NSTA) is the largest organization in the world committed to promoting excellence and innovation in science teaching and learning for all. NSTA's current membership of more than 53,000 includes science teachers, science supervisors, administrators, scientists, business and industry representatives, and others involved in and committed to science education. NSTA administers awards, grants, and student competitions to recognize the professional efforts of teachers and the innovative talents of their students.

## Eligibility

Outstanding educators who encourage innovation and student competitions that inspire creativity and reward team effort.

## Award

Programs include the Toyota TAPESTRY Grants for Teachers, the Craftsman NSTA Young Inventors Awards Program, Toshiba NSTA ExploraVision Awards, Shell Science Teaching Award, and the Robert Carleton Award, sponsored by Dow Chemical Company.

Teachers and students are awarded with:

- Cash awards, U.S. Savings bonds.
- School supplies and materials.
- Trips to the national convention and more.

## Application Process

There are many different grants, so it would be best to follow the links at the website for more information and application materials.

## Contact Information

National Science Teachers Association (NSTA)
1840 Wilson Boulevard
Arlington VA 22201-3000
Phone:      703-243-7100
Website:    www.nsta.org

# The Presidential Awards for Excellence in Mathematics and Science Teaching (PAEMST)

## Mission

Established in 1983 by the White House and sponsored by the National Science Foundation (NSF), this program identifies outstanding science and mathematics teachers in each state and the four U.S. jurisdictions to serve as models for their colleagues and become leaders in the improvement of science and mathematics education.

Since 1983, more than three thousand teachers have been selected to enter the network of Presidential Awardees. They represent a premier group of science and mathematics teachers who bring national and state standards to life in their classrooms. They provide the nation with an impressive array of expertise to help improve teaching and learning while becoming more deeply involved in activities such as curriculum materials selection, research, and teaching other teachers.

## Eligibility

- Certified teachers who are assigned to K–12 science and/or mathematics classrooms in a public or private school in a state or eligible jurisdiction.

- At least five years' K–12 teaching experience in science and/or mathematics prior to application.

- Full-time employees of their school districts.

- Elementary teachers who are assigned, at least half-time during the school year, to classroom teaching, and who teach mathematics and/or science in a self-contained classroom setting or as teaching specialists.

- Secondary teachers who are assigned, at least half-time during the school year, to classroom teaching of science or mathematics.

- Past Presidential Awardees are not eligible.

## Award

- $7,500 educational grant to the awardee for his or her school.

- A presidential citation.

- A trip to Washington, D.C., for a series of recognition events.

## Application Process

Applications are encouraged from teachers from all locations (urban, suburban, small town, rural) and all underrepresented minority groups (American Indians, African Americans, Hispanics, Native Alaskans, Native Pacific Islanders).

Each year, after the initial selection process at the state or territorial level, a national panel of distinguished scientists, mathematicians, and educators recommends teachers to receive a presidential award—one elementary and one secondary math teacher, and one elementary and one secondary science teacher from each jurisdiction. Application packets can be downloaded from the website.

## Contact Information

Presidential Awards for Excellence in Mathematics and Science Teaching
Directorate for Education and Human Resources
National Science Foundation
4201 Wilson Boulevard
Arlington, VA 22230
Phone:          703-306-0422
Website:        http://www.ehr.nsf.gov/pres_awards/proinfo1.shtm

# THE SHAKLEE TEACHER AWARD

## Mission

This award is designed to initiate positive changes in the education of children with disabilities by improving professional practice and influencing public policy. It recognizes up to ten of the country's most outstanding teachers of children with disabilities each year. The Shaklee Teacher Award is funded in part by Sigma Alpha Sorority, a national business women's organization of more than eight hundred members.

## Eligibility

Limited to professionals involved in direct teaching programs for children with disabilities.

## Award

- $1,000 cash award.

- Shaklee Teacher Award pewter sculpture designed by internationally acclaimed artist Michael Ricker.

- Four-day, small group learning experience led by members of the Shaklee Institute Senior Scholars Summer Session. All expenses, including travel, meals, and hotel accommodations, will be courtesy of the Shaklee Institute.

## Application Process

Teachers must describe numerous aspects of their competence as an educator and overall involvement within the field, show confidence in their effectiveness as professional educators, and seek meaningful development of their ability to contribute to their students and the profession.

Selection of these teachers is based on specific student outcomes and related contributions they have accomplished in their roles as teachers of children with disabilities. The standards reflected in this award exemplify the attributes of outstanding educators as determined by the Shaklee Institute Senior Scholars.

## Contact Information

Shaklee Institute for Improving Special Education
8700 East 29th Street North
Wichita, KS 67226
Phone:      316-634-8735
                 or
                 800-835-1043
Fax:          316-634-0555
Website:    http://www.shakleeinstitute.org/pages/teacher.htm

# THE WAL-MART GOOD WORKS
# TEACHER OF THE YEAR PROGRAM

## Mission

Our founder, Sam Walton, believed in servant-leadership, which makes our mission to serve our associates and customers with compassion and integrity. Our emphasis is on our associates, children, families, the local community, and other local programs that improve the quality of life in our communities with a specific focus on community education and scholarships.

## Eligibility

All public school teachers.

## Awards

- $500 grant at the community level.

- $5,000 grant for the State Teacher of the Year.

- $10,000 grant for the National Teacher of the Year.

## Application Process

Applications may be picked up at your local Wal-Mart, Neighborhood Market, or Sam's Club.

## Contact Information

Local Wal-Mart, Neighborhood Market, Sam's Club, or:

Wal-Mart Foundation
702 Southwest 8th Street
Bentonville, AR 72716-0150
Phone:          800-530-9925
Website:        http://www.walmartfoundation.org

# ABOUT THE AUTHORS

## Marsha Serling Goldberg

Born in Washington, D.C., Marsha Serling Goldberg was raised in Bethesda, Maryland, living a few years with her family in Ankara, Turkey, and Seoul, Korea.

After completing her undergraduate studies at the University of Vermont, she worked in Washington, D.C., as a dental hygienist before heading west to earn a Master of Science in Health Education from the University of Oregon. She is qualified by the Association for Psychological Type as a Myers-Briggs Type Indicator Trainer, is a graduate from the Western School of Feng Shui, and is a member of the International Feng Shui Guild. She conducts parent and adolescent workshops in the Pacific Northwest.

In a past life, or so it seems, before she did laundry daily for five growing sons, she taught at various levels from finger painting in preschool to health courses in college. She presently works as a Feng Shui practitioner and continues to provide laundry and food service for her large family. Marsha has always found parenting her most challenging and rewarding experience. She lives with her husband, Linn, and their children in Lake Oswego, Oregon.

# *Sonia Feldman*

Sonia Feldman was born in São Paulo, Brazil, and moved to the Washington, D.C., area at the age of eight. She graduated from the University of Maryland with a B.A. in Psychology and a minor in Art and Dance. After several years of teaching modern dance in the Boston area, Sonia began her career as a graphic designer. She eventually moved to Annapolis, Maryland, where she now lives with her husband, Jerry, and their two children. She has her own business: Sonia Feldman Communication Graphics.

Sonia enjoys having an office in a small historic town by the Chesapeake Bay and welcomes the opportunities that her design business provides. She particularly enjoys projects that combine her graphic design background with her interests in promoting the arts and education. She is very pleased that *Teachers with Class* provides her with an opportunity to contribute to the support and recognition that educators deserve.

Marsha and Sonia have remained close friends since the day they met—their first day of junior high school in Bethesda, Maryland.

**Do you have a teacher you would like to honor?**

Please visit our website at www.teacherswithclass.com and
send your special-teacher story to story@teacherswithclass.com.